Barack Obama

A Life of Leadership

By Rachael Morlock

Portions of this book originally appeared in
Barack Obama by Michael V. Uschan.

LUCENT
P R E S S

Published in 2020 by
Lucent Press, an Imprint of Greenhaven Publishing, LLC
353 3rd Avenue
Suite 255
New York, NY 10010

Designer: Deanna Paternostro
Editor: Rachael Morlock

Cataloging-in-Publication Data

Names: Morlock, Rachael.
Title: Barack Obama: a life of leadership / Rachael Morlock.
Description: New York : Lucent Press, 2020. | Series: People in the news |
Includes index.
Identifiers: ISBN 9781534568402 (pbk.) | ISBN 9781534568419 (library bound) |
ISBN 9781534568426 (ebook)
Subjects: LCSH: Obama, Barack–Juvenile literature. | Presidents–United States–
Biography–Juvenile literature.
Classification: LCC E908.M67 2020 | DDC 973.932092 B–dc23

Printed in China

Some of the images in this book illustrate individuals who are models. The
depictions do not imply actual situations or events.

CPSIA compliance information: Batch #BW20KL: For further information contact Greenhaven Publishing LLC, New York,
New York, at 1-844-317-7404.

Contents

Foreword

We live in a world where the latest news is always available and where it seems we have unlimited access to the lives of the people in the news. Entire television networks are devoted to news about politics, sports, and entertainment. Social media has allowed people to have an unprecedented level of interaction with celebrities. We have more information at our fingertips than ever before. However, how much do we really know about the people we see on television news programs, social media feeds, and magazine covers?

Despite the constant stream of news, the full stories behind the lives of some of the world's most newsworthy men and women are often unknown. Who was Lady Gaga before she became a star? What does LeBron James do when he is not playing basketball? What inspires Lin-Manuel Miranda?

This series aims to answer questions like these about some of the biggest names in pop culture, sports, politics, and technology. While the subjects of this series come from all walks of life and areas of expertise, they share a common magnetism that has made them all captivating figures in the public eye. They have shaped the world in some unique way, and—in many cases—they are poised to continue to shape the world for many years to come.

These biographies are not just a collection of basic facts. They tell compelling stories that show how each figure grew to become a powerful public personality. Each book aims to paint a complete, realistic picture of its subject—from the challenges they overcame to the controversies they caused. In doing so, each book reinforces the idea that even the most famous faces on the news are real people who are much more complex than we are often shown in brief video clips or sound bites. Readers are also reminded that there is even more to a person than what they present to the world through social media posts, press releases, and interviews. The whole story of a person's life can only be discovered by digging beneath the surface of their public persona, and that is what this series allows readers to do.

The books in this series are filled with enlightening quotes from speeches and interviews given by the subjects, as well as quotes and anecdotes from those who know their story best: family, friends, coaches, and colleagues. All quotes are noted to provide guidance for further research. Detailed lists of additional resources are also included, as are timelines, indexes, and unique photographs. These text features come together to enhance the reading experience and encourage readers to dive deeper into the stories of these influential men and women.

Fame can be fleeting, but the subjects featured in this series have real staying power. They have fundamentally impacted their respective fields and have achieved great success through hard work and true talent. They are men and women defined by their accomplishments, and they are often seen as role models for the next generation. They have left their mark on the world in a major way, and their stories are meant to inspire readers to leave their mark, too.

Introduction

Making History

In 2008, an eager coalition of first-time, young, and minority voters went to the polls to elect the president of the United States. They vaulted a candidate named Barack Obama to victory with almost 70 million votes. Obama had appealed to this unprecedented alliance of voters with his fervent calls for hope and change in their country. For the next eight years, Obama served the United States as president and worked to bring about the changes he promised. His presidency was marked with both advances and defeats, and progress was at turns slow or substantial. However, by the end of his presidency in 2017, Obama had left an undeniable mark on the nation. His achievements as an individual were great, but as a leader, they were also symbolic.

Obama's Oath

On January 20, 2009, Obama took the oath of office as the 44th president of the United States of America. Obama's short but elegant inaugural address was somber because of the immense problems he would face as president, from the nation's worst economic crisis since the Great Depression in the 1920s and 1930s to ongoing wars in Iraq and Afghanistan. However, Obama's

The large, record-breaking crowd at Obama's 2009 inauguration flooded across the National Mall as the new president took office.

speech was also filled with hope that the nation could and would conquer those crises as it had so many others in its past. Obama declared:

Forty-four Americans have now taken the presidential oath. The words have been spoken during rising tides of prosperity and the still waters of peace. Yet, every so often the oath is taken amidst gathering clouds and raging storms. At these moments, America has carried on not simply because of the skill or vision of those in high office, but because We the People have remained faithful to the ideals of our forbears, and true to our founding documents. So it has been. So it must be with this generation of Americans.[1]

Obama spoke on the west steps of the Capitol. From there, his words echoed through loudspeakers across Washington's National Mall, which stretches 1.9 miles (3 km) from the Capitol to the Lincoln Memorial. They were heard by a record inaugural crowd of 1.8 million people, who had traveled from every state and many countries around the world to witness history being made.

In addition to being the 44th president and a symbol of hope for a troubled country, Obama was also the first African American president of the United States. His election was historically significant because it was the fulfillment of a most sacred ideal expressed by America's founders in the Declaration of Independence, the document that declares to the entire world, "We hold these truths to be self-evident, that all men are created equal."[2] On the day a black man became president, those words seemed to be truer than ever before in the nation's history.

Steps Toward Equality

When Thomas Jefferson wrote the Declaration of Independence in 1776, a half-million black men, women, and children were enslaved and did not share in that promise of equality. The United States failed to extend equality to millions of African Americans, and slavery continued until the end of the American Civil War nine decades later in 1865. The Capitol building that loomed behind Obama as he spoke was itself a grim relic of the nation's past—it was built largely by enslaved laborers, as was the White House, the presidential home in which Obama and his family would live.

Those historic buildings, however, were not the only bitter reminders of slavery that day in the nation's capital. The National Mall, on which nearly 2 million people gathered to witness Obama's inauguration, had once been the site of slave markets in which African Americans were bought and sold. Slavery is also intimately connected to the presidency itself. George Washington, the nation's first president, was a slave owner, as were several other presidents, including Thomas Jefferson and Andrew Jackson. Many cooks and servants in the White House were enslaved, and the second child born in the White House was the child of two enslaved people named Fanny and Eddy.

In addition, many people in the giant inaugural crowd were descendants of enslaved Americans, including the new president's wife, Michelle, and daughters, Malia and Sasha. The new First Lady's great-great-grandfather had toiled as a slave on a South Carolina rice plantation before the Civil War.

Even after slavery was abolished, many whites still considered African Americans inferior and used racist laws to deny them basic rights. For another century, black people in many states were denied one of the most basic and important rights citizens have—the right to vote. Other laws barred them from entering restaurants, stores, and even public bathrooms because these places were reserved for whites.

Black people were denied their civil rights and any chance for equality until the civil rights movement in the 1950s and 1960s. The movement was waged by black leaders like Martin Luther King Jr. and tens of thousands of African Americans and white supporters. The dramatic protests they staged to confront racist officials and citizens in Southern states finally forced the federal government to pass legislation that outlawed racial discrimination and protected the rights of African Americans.

Obama is not a descendant of slaves. His ancestors lived in Africa until his father came to the United States in 1959.

However, in his inaugural address, Obama talked about the discrimination that his father might have faced upon arriving in America because of racism. He said that the nation's work is to end injustice and fulfill the high ideals that the United States is founded on:

> *This is the meaning of our liberty and our creed, why men and women and children of every race and every faith can join in celebration across this magnificent mall. And why a man whose father less than 60 years ago might not have been served at a local restaurant can now stand before you to take a most sacred oath.*[3]

Free at Last!

In a coincidence of history, Obama's inauguration came one day after the annual national holiday to honor Martin Luther King Jr. People who came to witness the inauguration were gathered in the same place where King had given his own historic speech more than three decades earlier. On August 28, 1963, King told 250,000 black and white people who had assembled to protest racism that he had a dream. King said he longed to see the time "when all of God's children, black men and white men, Jews and Gentiles, Protestants and Catholics, will be able to join hands and sing in the words of the old Negro spiritual, 'Free at last! Free at last! Thank God Almighty, we are free at last.'"[4]

Reverend Rick Warren was one of many people at Obama's inauguration who remembered King's famous words. In a formal prayer before Obama was sworn in as president, Warren said, "We know today that Dr. King and a great cloud of witnesses are shouting [with joy] in heaven."[5] Like many people, Warren believed Obama's election was a sign that King's dream was finally coming true.

Getting Started

Obama's inauguration day in 2009 was the culmination of a long journey that started with his childhood in Hawaii. It progressed through his success as a student at Columbia and Harvard, and it was renewed through his dedication to serving communities in Chicago, Illinois. After only two years in the U.S. Senate, Obama continued his journey by capturing the hopes and imaginations of millions of Americans. A long and absorbing campaign led Obama to the steps of the Capitol, and at his inauguration, Obama's work for America truly began.

Chapter One

Humble Beginnings

During his early days in life, Barack Obama's eventual launch to power would have seemed surprising. Unlike other leaders born into families with wealth and powerful connections, Obama came from humble origins. He is from a mix of cultures and backgrounds unusual within mainstream America. Although his adversaries later searched for weaknesses connected with this background, Obama's unique personal history has largely been a strength. Overcoming the challenges of understanding and accepting his personal identity prepared Obama for many of the difficulties he would face as a public figure. In addition, his broad appeal to a diverse range of people in the United States and abroad helped Obama form connections and call for unity across the globe.

Two Countries, Two Worlds

Barack Hussein Obama Jr. is the son of two people from vastly different parts of the world. His father, Barack Obama Sr., was from Kenya. He was born a member of the Luo tribe on the shores of Lake Victoria in a place called Alego. His mother, S. Ann Dunham, was born in Kansas.

Obama's Birth Certificate

On August 21, 1959, Hawaii became the 50th addition to the United States of America. Barack Obama was born in the relatively new state on August 4, 1961, two years later. Since the United States Constitution grants citizenship to all individuals born on U.S. soil, Obama became a citizen the moment he was born.

When Obama was seeking the presidency, rumors circulated that he was not an American citizen. American citizenship is a requirement in order to serve as president. The rumor that Obama was actually born in Kenya, Indonesia, or another country was promoted by some Republicans, including future president Donald J. Trump. As a result, a large number of people began to believe the rumors. These "birthers," as they came to be called, demanded to see Obama's birth certificate to verify his eligibility for the presidency. Obama released his birth certificate in 2008, but it failed to crush the rumors. A copy of his birth certificate can still be viewed on the White House archives website.

A bright child, Barack Obama Sr. tended goats on his father's farm until he earned a sponsorship to attend a university in the United States. In 1959, at the age of 23, he became the University of Hawaii's first African student. It was there that he met 18-year-old Dunham, who was also a student at the university.

Dunham was a smart but shy only child. She was actually named Stanley Ann, after her father, Stanley Dunham, a man whose interests and energy led their small family to move around the country frequently as he sought better jobs and a better way of life. Born and raised in Kansas, Stanley Dunham (or "Gramps," as young Barack called him) was a soldier in World War II who never experienced combat. Ann was born at the army base where he was stationed. Upon his return to civilian life, he enrolled at the University of California, Berkeley, under the GI bill, which provides tuition to military veterans. However, according to Barack in his memoir, *Dreams from My Father: A Story of Race and Inheritance*, "The classroom couldn't contain his ambitions."[6] So the family moved again, first back to Kansas, then through a series of small Texas towns, and eventually to Seattle, where they stayed long enough for Ann to finish high school.

During that time, Stanley Dunham worked as a furniture salesman. One day, he learned from his manager that the furniture company was opening a new store in Honolulu, Hawaii. That bit of news led to a fateful decision to move in 1959, this time off the mainland of the United States to a so-called island paradise where, Dunham believed, an enterprising young man could make his mark. Barack described his grandfather's character: "He would always be like that, my grandfather, always searching for that new start, always running away from the familiar … His was an American character, one typical of men of his generation, men who embraced the notion of freedom and individualism and the open road."[7]

Despite Stanley Dunham's ambitions, he never got rich. His wife, Madelyn, also worked. She had a job in a bank and rose up in the ranks through hard work and professionalism. When Stanley experienced low points in business, Madelyn kept the family afloat financially.

Cultural Divides

Although the Dunhams never prospered, they did provide Ann with a stable home. They were open-minded parents, but their tolerance was tested when 18-year-old Ann informed them that she wanted to marry a 23-year-old black man from another continent. Yet neither Stanley nor Madelyn could deny that Ann

The Right to Marry

Although civil rights were expanded in the United States during the 1960s, interracial marriage was by no means easily accepted. If Ann Dunham and Barack Obama Sr. had met on the mainland of the United States, they might not have married. In many states, it was still illegal for whites and blacks to marry. And in the Southern states at the time, it's likely that Obama Sr. could have been harmed, even hanged, for having a relationship with a white woman.

In fact, it was not until Barack Obama Jr. was six years old that the U.S. Supreme Court declared Virginia's Racial Integrity Act of 1924 unconstitutional in the case of *Loving v. Virginia*. This legally ended all race-based restrictions on marriage in the United States. At the time these laws were ruled unconstitutional, 16 states still prohibited interracial marriage. The ruling wasn't completely effective until November 2000, when Alabama became the last state to repeal its law.

was truly in love, and Barack Obama Sr.'s intelligence and charm quickly won them over.

Barack Obama Sr.'s father, Hussein, was less agreeable to the match. Shortly before the wedding, he wrote a letter to Stanley Dunham from Africa saying that he did not approve of the marriage. One reason for this, according to Ann, was that Hussein did not want the Obama blood to be "sullied by a white woman."[8] Barack Obama Sr. wrote back to Hussein informing him that he was going forward with the wedding. He married Ann in a small civil ceremony in 1960. Barack Hussein Obama Jr. was born shortly after on August 4, 1961.

Barack Obama Sr. continued with his education. Upon graduation from the University of Hawaii with a degree in economics earned in only three years, he received two scholarships for graduate school. One was from the New School in New York City and would have provided him with full tuition, along with room and board for Ann and the baby. The second scholarship, from Harvard University in Massachusetts, provided only full tuition for Obama Sr. According to Ann, while deciding which offer to accept, Obama Sr. received harsh news from his father. Hussein was adamant in his rejection of Ann. He threatened to have his son's student visa revoked, which would have forced Obama Sr. to return to Africa before completing his graduate studies. The pressure from Hussein, coupled with his own overwhelming desire to attend Harvard, led Obama Sr. to choose the Ivy League school. He left for Massachusetts in 1963 to pursue his studies. Ann remained in Hawaii with their two-year-old son. The couple eventually divorced.

Thus, early in his life, Barack Jr. was different from other children in many ways. Half-black, half-white, and distant from his father, he already could not be neatly categorized into one ethnicity or demographic.

Life Abroad

Barack's life soon took another turn. About two years after the senior Obama left, Ann met Lolo Soetoro. He was a University of Hawaii student from Indonesia, a Southeast Asian country comprising several islands in the Indian and Pacific Oceans. After dating Soetoro for two years, Ann accepted his proposal of marriage. Soon after the couple married, Soetoro returned to his homeland, but unlike Barack Obama Sr., he took his new bride and her now six-year-old son with him. Barack, who was called "Barry" as a child, lived in Indonesia for four years. There, his mother gave birth to his half sister, Maya.

While living in Indonesia, Barack came to understand how the United States, unlike many other countries, offers numerous opportunities as an economically free society. Even as a young child, he observed that people in Indonesia were born into families whose lot in life was dictated by their economic class. It was extremely difficult to ascend into a higher economic class. In

While living in Indonesia, Barack Obama studied for four years at an elementary school in Jakarta. He is circled here in this class photo from 1969

the American ideal, by contrast, all people have the freedoms of life, liberty, and the pursuit of happiness regardless of their race, gender, or class.

Barack was also exposed to poverty in Indonesia, where many families struggled daily to obtain enough food. People lived modestly in ramshackle homes where it was common to see chickens and livestock roaming in yards. Later in life, Barack drew parallels between what he witnessed in Indonesia and what he witnessed in American inner cities.

During his time in Indonesia, Barack also began to learn about his African American heritage. His mother regularly provided him with reading materials about the treatment of African Americans in the United States. She taught him about the nation's history of slavery and the more recent fight for civil rights. She made sure that her son knew of the great contributions made by black leaders in politics, history, culture, music, and sports. Obama described her message in his memoir: "To be black was to be the beneficiary of a great inheritance, a special destiny, glorious burdens that only we were strong enough to bear."[9]

However, the pride his mother passed on to young Barack was counteracted by his growing awareness of issues surrounding race. Most disturbing was the self-hatred among some African Americans due to their skin color. Barack came upon the subject while reading a *Life* magazine story about a black man who had tried to peel off his skin to look white. It had never occurred to Barack that people would feel so ashamed of their skin color that they would take such dangerous steps, but the article changed his understanding of race. He explained in his memoir, "I began to notice … that there was nobody like me in the Sears, Roebuck Christmas catalog that Toot [his grandmother] and Gramps sent us, and that Santa was a white man … I still trusted my mother's love—but I now faced the prospect that her account of the world, and my father's place in it, was somehow incomplete."[10]

Return to Hawaii

After four years of living in Indonesia, Barack was sent back to Hawaii to live with Toot and Gramps and enter fifth grade at Punahou Academy, an elite Hawaiian prep school. His grandparents were only too happy to accommodate him. They were proud that their grandchild was a student at such a well-respected educational institution.

Having been away from the United States for so long, Barack felt out of place at Punahou. The majority of other students had attended school together since kindergarten. Most of them came from well-to-do families and had better-quality and more stylish clothes than Barack. He was one of only two black children in his class, and other students mocked his foreign name. Instead of feeling proud of his Kenyan heritage, Barack often felt conflicted, even embarrassed by his differences from the other children.

Obama and his sister, Maya (shown here in 2008), lived apart for long stretches of their early life. Obama returned to live with his grandparents in Hawaii when Maya was still very young.

As Barack sought to fit in among his classmates, he received some startling news. Obama Sr. had been in a serious car accident in Kenya, and he was coming for a month-long visit to recover.

Father and Son

The young Barack was nervous about meeting his father. His mother and grandparents had told him that his father was a brilliant diplomat doing important work to help his country, but Barack still felt he knew little about him. Sometimes he felt proud that his father was a leader in Kenya trying to improve life for his countrymen. But at other times, Barack could not understand why his father was not with him.

The visit was awkward and confusing. Barack was impressed with his father, but the man was a stranger to him. The boy knew that his father was intelligent and worldly, but he was also strict, criticizing his son for watching too much television and for not studying more. Education had been the key to Obama Sr.'s escape from an impoverished life. Barack was not as desperate to learn as his father had been, and this led to tension during their brief time together.

The elder Obama's visit created tension for his son in another way as well. Young Barack had grown up different, a black child being raised by white grandparents in a state populated by Hawaiians. He feared that being exposed as the son of an African who spoke with a strange accent would only emphasize the contrast between himself and other children in Hawaii.

One event in particular characterized the conflicted emotions that Barack had for his father. When Barack's teacher learned that his father was visiting, she invited him to speak to her class. Barack dreaded the day because he expected his classmates to tease him afterward. His fear turned to pride, however, as the man from Africa held the students transfixed. Barack described what happened:

> He spoke of the wild animals that still roamed the plains, the tribes that still required a young boy to kill a lion to prove his manhood … He told us of Kenya's struggle to be free, how the British had wanted to stay and unjustly rule the people, just as they had in America; how they had been enslaved only because of the color of their skin, just as they had in America; but that Kenyans … longed to be free and develop themselves through hard work and sacrifice.[11]

Barack's father stayed for only one month. Soon after his father returned to Africa, Barack's mother, now separated from Soetoro, came back to Hawaii to pursue a master's degree in anthropology. Barack lived in an apartment a block from the Punahou Academy with his mother and sister for the next three years.

Life in Kenya

After Barack Obama Sr. divorced Ann Dunham and returned to Africa, he married a white woman whose father worked in the Kenyan embassy. For some time, he did well working for an American oil company. Kenya gained its independence from England in 1963, and Obama Sr. was connected with all the top government people, which led him to take a high-ranking job with the Ministry of Tourism.

Obama Sr. was still with the Ministry of Tourism in 1966, when a division grew between two Kenyan tribes: the Kikuyu, led by President Jomo Kenyatta, and the Luo, Obama Sr.'s tribe. The Luo tribe complained that Kikuyu tribe members were getting the best jobs in the country, and Obama Sr. protested publicly about the issue. His outspokenness caused him to be banished from the government. His passport was revoked, and he could not leave Kenya. During this time, his wife left him. He began to drink and fell into near poverty for many years.

Eventually, the political situation in Kenya changed, and Obama Sr. was able to return to government work in the Ministry of Finance. Tragically, just as his life was beginning to improve, he was killed in a car accident in 1982, when Obama Jr. was 21.

Becoming Barack

When his mother made plans to return to Indonesia once again—this time to complete fieldwork for her graduate degree—Barack elected to stay at Punahou and live with his grandparents. Barack's internal conflicts about his identity grew during these years. His heritage created conflict when he befriended blacks who voiced their resentment of whites, not knowing that Barack's mother was white. In an interview with talk-show host Oprah Winfrey, Obama described his inner turmoil:

> *There was a level of ... a divided identity. One that was inside the home and one was to the outside world ... And I think it was reconciling those two things, the understanding that I can be African American and proud of that heritage and proud of that culture and part of that community and yet not be limited by it. And that ... that's not exclusive of my love for my mother or my love for my grandparents, that I can be part of the same thing.*[12]

Barack's personal conflicts along with typical teen rebelliousness led him to wayward behavior. He drank and smoked, developing a cigarette habit that would plague him for years.

Barack frequently sought refuge on the basketball court. He recalled:

> *I was living out a caricature of black male adolescence, itself a caricature of swaggering American manhood ... At least on the basketball court I could find a community of sorts, with an inner life all its own. It was there that I would make my closest white friends, on turf where blackness couldn't be a disadvantage.*[13]

As Barack spent more time on social activities than academics, his grades suffered a bit, and so did his ambition. He drifted without clear direction as his high school years concluded.

Off to College

Despite his lack of focus on the future, Barack wound up at Occidental College in Los Angeles, California, in 1979. The criteria he used to pick the school was based on a whim. He chose Occidental because he had heard of the school from a girl vacationing in Hawaii from Brentwood, a Los Angeles suburb.

Obama claimed that he found acceptance and belonging on the basketball court, first playing pickup basketball in park playgrounds near his home and then as a member of his high school basketball team (shown here).

In college in California, Obama continued to explore his identity and the possibilities for his future.

At Occidental, he once again grappled with issues of race. Unlike the black students from economically depressed cities, Barack could not easily identify with the plight of impoverished and disadvantaged black people in the United States. In fact, he reflected in his memoir that he was more like "the black students who had grown up in the suburbs, kids whose parents had already paid the price of escape"[14] from inner cities. His multiracial makeup compounded his sense of estrangement from black people, yet he was not comfortable downplaying or even disavowing his African American heritage as some multiracial students did.

Once again, Barack reached a crossroads. On one hand, he tried to assimilate what he presumed to be black thinking—rebel against white authority, even if it means doing poorly in college. However, he also encountered black students who appreciated the sacrifices their families had made to send them to school, and they criticized him for not applying himself academically. Writer and reporter Noam Scheiber stated, "Obama's eventual response to his multicultural background was neither to shun his black identity, nor to shore it up by segregating himself from whites. It was to be racially proud, while striving to succeed in mainstream (and predominantly white) institutions."[15]

Eventually, Barack realized that he was not living up to his full potential. After two years at Occidental, he transferred to Columbia University in New York City in 1981. His childhood and adolescence over, Barack set out to find his calling. He was eager to embrace the new realities of life in New York City and increase his knowledge and understanding of the world.

Chapter **Two**

An American Experience

O bama's reflective and curious nature led him to search for answers about his place in the world. It also opened his eyes to the similar struggles of people across America who were trying to define and assert their identity. From New York City to Chicago, Illinois, Obama listened to these individuals and communities. He looked for ways to use his talents and intelligence not only to clarify his own voice but also to amplify the voices of others.

A New Direction

As a young adult, Obama made a series of career moves that were impressive yet unexpected. He arrived at Columbia University eager to live in what he called "a true city, with black neighborhoods in close proximity."[16] Columbia is located only a few blocks from Harlem, a section of New York City that is home to thousands of African Americans. It also exposed Obama to many of the problems common to urban areas: poverty, drugs, violence, and homelessness.

By the time Obama completed his degree in political science with a specialization in international relations in 1983, he had decided to become a community organizer. He wanted to bring people together on a local level to promote social progress and protest unfair treatment. Obama could focus on any of the problems facing communities, including poor educational facilities, inferior housing conditions, pollution, lost jobs, and low wages for working-class citizens. According to Obama, "Communities had never been a given in this country ... Communities had to be created, fought for, tended like gardens."[17]

Community Organizing

Despite the fact that American citizens in inner cities had many problems, it was not so simple for Obama to find work as a community organizer. He submitted letters to many civil rights organizations and to black elected officials all over the country who had progressive agendas, yet no one replied.

To earn an income in the meantime, he took a research assistant job at a consulting house for a multinational corporation. He was eventually promoted to the position of financial writer. Obama now had money, his own office, and his own secretary. He described this time in his life in his memoir:

> Sometimes coming out of an interview with Japanese financiers or German bond traders, I would catch my reflection in the elevator doors—see myself in a suit and tie, a briefcase in my hand—and for a split second I would imagine myself as a captain of industry, barking out orders, closing the deal, before I remembered who it was that I had told myself I wanted to be and felt pangs of guilt for my own lack of resolve.[18]

This guilt eventually led Obama to resign his position and focus again on finding work as a community organizer. Although he got a job organizing a conference on drugs, unemployment, and housing, this role was too removed from the streets. So he took another position, this time in Harlem, trying to convince the students at City College of the importance of recycling. Then, he took another low-paying assignment passing out flyers for an assemblyman's race in Brooklyn. "In six months I was broke, unemployed, eating soup from a can,"[19] he recalled. Finally, though, an opportunity came to him that redirected his life.

Getting to Work

Obama was recruited by a labor organizer affiliated with the Calumet Community Religious Conference (CCRC), an organization formed to address the impact of factory closings and layoffs then taking place in South Chicago. Once critical to the nation's economy, Chicago's manufacturing companies had relocated operations—mostly overseas to take advantage of cheaper labor—or had simply gone out of business. The CCRC sought to mobilize residents through a network of 28 suburban and urban churches, known as the Developing Communities Project (DCP). The objective was to bring jobs and manufacturing back to Chicago. Obama was hired in 1985 to help unite people in this common cause.

Obama found that his job was not easy. For one, he discovered that it was difficult to convince local black religious leaders to speak out for more and better jobs for African Americans. This was partly because the mayor of Chicago at the time was Harold Washington, the first African American ever elected to that position. Washington was a hero to Chicago's African Americans, and some of the church leaders did not want to be perceived as disrespectful to him.

Despite the reluctance of some leaders to cooperate, Obama pressed on with a variety of issues that strayed somewhat from the mission of the DCP. He held a meeting to address gang violence, but the organized event flopped. Hardly anyone showed up. Obama learned that gang violence was a difficult issue to rally people around. While people certainly wanted something to be done to improve safety in their neighborhoods, they most wanted help finding jobs. Obama learned a valuable lesson: If he was going to succeed at community organizing, he had to focus on concrete matters, such as jobs and decent housing for the working poor. Soon, he found a place to concentrate his efforts: Altgeld Gardens.

Hope for Housing

Obama realized his first real success as a community organizer by helping to call the attention of the Mayor's Office of Employment and Training (MET) to Altgeld Gardens. This was a public housing project on the southern edge of the city of Chicago. Unlike high-rise projects common to most major cities, Altgeld was only two stories tall. Although the residents did not own their apartments and were surrounded by difficult conditions, they took pride in their homes. Obama described Altgeld:

> The Altgeld Gardens Public Housing Project sat at Chicago's southernmost edge: 2,000 apartments arranged in a series of two-story brick buildings with army-green doors and grimy mock shutters … To the east … was the Lake Calumet landfill, the largest in the Midwest. And to the north, directly across the street, was the Metropolitan Sanitary District's sewage treatment plant … The stench, the toxins, the empty uninhabited landscape. For close to a century, the few square miles surrounding Altgeld had taken in the offal of scores of factories, the price people had paid for their high-wage jobs. Now that the jobs were gone, and those people that could had already left, it seemed only natural to use the land as a dump. A dump—and a place to house poor blacks.[20]

Obama interviewed and befriended residents of Altgeld and learned that employment was a key issue for them. He set out to connect the group with MET, which referred unemployed people to training programs throughout the city. He discovered that MET did not have an office anywhere near Altgeld, so he wrote to the woman in charge of the agency. She agreed to meet with a group of Altgeld Gardens residents. Obama's goal was to get a job intake and training center on the far south side of the city. He coached

Obama reached a new phase in his work as a community organizer when he made connections with the residents of Chicago's Altgeld Gardens housing project (shown here).

the residents on what to say at the meeting and made all the arrangements for it. More than 100 people attended the event, and the director of MET could not deny that an office needed to be established in the community.

Battling Asbestos

Emboldened by his triumph with MET, Obama's next challenge involved helping Altgeld residents persuade the city of Chicago to fix a problem with asbestos. Asbestos was once considered a useful product because of its fireproof quality. For decades, asbestos was used to insulate pipes and walls in buildings and homes until it was discovered to cause cancer. A woman from the Altgeld housing project told Obama of her concern that the apartments could contain asbestos.

Obama led a small contingent of residents to the building manager's office and was told that the apartments had been tested and that there was no asbestos in them. When pressed for evidence, the building manager could not deliver proof of this testing. In response, Obama and some Altgeld residents organized a bus trip to the Community Housing Authority's offices.

Obama notified the press to attend the meeting because he knew that the news media would be interested in a story about the possibility of a known cancer-causing material such as asbestos having a negative impact on the health of city residents. He was also confident that Community Housing Authority executives would not want to be portrayed publicly as negligent. Sure enough, with cameras rolling, they admitted that asbestos was present in the apartments of Altgeld Gardens. City officials immediately proposed a plan to remove the asbestos.

Obama felt triumphant as a result of this win and reflected on it in his memoir:

> I changed as a result of that bus trip … It was the sort of change that's important not because it alters your concrete circumstances in some way … but because it hints at what might be possible and therefore spurs you on, beyond the immediate exhilaration, beyond any subsequent disappointments, to retrieve that thing that you once, ever so briefly, held in your hand. That bus ride kept me going, I think. Maybe it still does.[21]

Harvard Bound

Although Obama began to experience more victories than defeats in Chicago, he believed that he needed additional education to become more effective as a leader. After several years as a community organizer, he applied to law school.

As he had hoped, Obama was accepted into Harvard Law School. Before leaving for Boston, Massachusetts, to attend

Obama followed in his father's footsteps when he accepted an invitation to study at Harvard.

Harvard, Obama traveled to Kenya to learn more about his family. He spent time with aunts, uncles, and cousins whom he met for the first time, and he had the opportunity to meet his Kenyan grandmother, Sarah Onyango Obama. All of these relatives told him stories of his father and grandfather. According to author and acquaintance Scott Turow, it was in Kenya that Obama "managed to fully embrace a heritage and a family he'd never fully known and come to terms with his father."[22]

Upon his return from Kenya in 1988, Obama entered Harvard Law School. He excelled there and became the first African American president of the prestigious *Harvard Law Review* in 1990. During this time, his potential as a political leader was obvious. In an article in *TIME* magazine, his former professor Laurence Tribe stated, "I've known Senators, Presidents. I've never known anyone with what seems to me more raw political talent. He [Obama] just seems to have the surest way of calmly reaching across what are impenetrable barriers to many people."[23]

While on summer leave from Harvard to work at a Chicago firm, Obama met Michelle Robinson. Robinson, also a graduate of Harvard Law School, had earned her undergraduate degree at Princeton University. She came from a working-class African American family in Chicago. *New Yorker* staff writer William Finnegan states, "[Obama] turned out to have little interest in corporate law but plenty of interest in Michelle."[24] After their engagement, Obama visited Kenya again, this time with Robinson.

A plaque in Chicago marks the spot where Barack and Michelle Obama shared their first kiss.

First Presidency

Published since 1887, the *Harvard Law Review* is one of the most prestigious journals of legal scholarship in the United States. It was created by Louis Brandeis, a Harvard Law School alumnus and Boston attorney who went on to become a justice on the U.S. Supreme Court. The purpose of the *Harvard Law Review* is to be an effective research tool for practicing lawyers and students of the law. Additionally, it provides opportunities for law students to write their own articles, which typically take the form of comments about cases or recent court decisions. Run by students, the monthly *Harvard Law Review* averages 2,000 pages per volume and reaches 8,000 subscribers, an audience comprising attorneys, judges, and professors.

Each year, about 10 student candidates run for the position of president of the *Harvard Law Review*. Staff of the review then elect the candidate best qualified to lead the publication. It is an extremely competitive process. Before Barack Obama, no African American had ever attained the position.

Obama's career path from Harvard to the White House was one of historic firsts. Here, he poses in the *Harvard Law Review* office.

Obama graduated magna cum laude (with highest honors) from Harvard Law School in 1991 and was sought after by several prominent law firms. Moreover, Abner Mikva, a former five-term congressman for Illinois who was chief judge of the U.S. Court of Appeals for the D.C. circuit, tried to recruit Obama as a clerk, a position that could have led to work with the Supreme Court. However, Obama turned down the offer. Unlike many people in his situation who would have chosen the pursuit of money and power, Obama wanted to return to the roots he had put down on Chicago's South Side.

Politics in Chicago

After graduating from Harvard Law School, Obama married Michelle Robinson in 1992. The ceremony was bittersweet for the couple: Michelle's father died before he could give his daughter away, and Gramps, Barack's maternal grandfather, had recently lost his life to prostate cancer. The newlyweds moved into the Hyde Park neighborhood on Chicago's South Side. They eventually had two daughters: Malia, born in 1998, and Sasha, born in 2001.

As a Chicago resident once again, Obama became director of the Illinois Project Vote, helping to register 100,000 mostly minority, low-income Democratic voters from April to November 1992. His efforts helped Bill Clinton carry Illinois in the 1992 presidential election and helped Carol Moseley Braun become the first African American woman to be elected to the U.S. Senate.

A small, public-interest law firm hired Obama in 1993. There, he worked as a civil rights attorney, specializing in employment discrimination, fair housing, and voting-rights litigation. That same year he was named in *Crain's* magazine's list of "40 under 40" outstanding young leaders in the city of Chicago. He also became a lecturer at the University of Chicago Law School.

Three years later, Obama launched his political career. In 1996, he ran for and won election to the Illinois state senate. As a state senator, Obama focused his efforts on helping working families. One way he did this was to collaborate with Democrats and Republicans alike to create programs, such as the state earned-income tax credit. The refundable tax credit reduces or eliminates the amount of taxes that low-income people pay. In three years, this program provided more than $100 million in tax cuts to families in Illinois. Obama also pushed through an expansion of early childhood education and helped broaden a state health insurance program for children who were otherwise uninsured.

Learning from Defeat

After nearly four years of serving as a state senator, Obama attempted to become a member of the U.S. House of Representatives by running against incumbent Bobby Rush in 2000. Rush was active during the civil rights movement of the 1960s and was popular among local residents. In 1968, he helped found the Illinois Black Panther Party, a radical group whose occasional militaristic activities attracted the attention of the government and local law enforcement. Rush, however, had also helped his fellow inner-city residents through peaceful and law-abiding means. His record showed improvements in health care and the environment, as well as the passage of strong gun control measures and the implementation of programs that spurred economic development.

Indeed, Rush had been successful in accomplishing many of the social reforms that Obama had been seeking to enact. Yet more important than Rush's seniority and track record was the perceptual advantage he held over Obama. According to Noam Scheiber, Rush frequently intimated that Obama was not "black enough … that he [had not] been around the first congressional district long enough to really see what's going on,"[25] and that Obama was an elitist. There was little Obama could do to reverse these perceptions, and Rush defeated him, receiving 61 percent of the vote to Obama's 30 percent.

Lessons from the State Senate

After losing to Rush, Obama refocused his attention and talents in the Illinois state senate. Yet even there he suffered a

Obama took a chance in running against established politician Bobby Rush in the 2000 congressional election.

significant political setback. The Republicans were prepared to fight strongly against a gun control bill, and the Democrats needed Obama's skills and influence to help their side. Obama was in Hawaii visiting relatives as the vote approached, and his younger daughter became sick. Torn between obligations to his family and to the state senate, Obama chose to stay in Hawaii with his daughter. The bill was defeated. Obama's explanation for his absence, according to Turow, "did not play either with the press ... or his fellow politicians, who'd left plenty of sickbeds and vacations in their time for the sake of public duty."[26]

Nevertheless, Obama carried on in the state senate. He worked to make sure that certain ethnic or minority groups were not unfairly targeted for criminal prosecution and to prevent wrongful convictions in death-penalty cases. After a number of inmates on death row were found innocent, Obama, with the help of law enforcement officials, drafted legislation that required the videotaping of interrogations and confessions in all murder cases. Even as opponents cited the plan as too costly for most police departments, Obama's proposal was approved.

Obama remained fearless in embracing unpopular causes. He wrote and worked hard to gather support from both political parties for a bill that required law enforcement personnel to keep track of the race of drivers they pulled over for traffic stops. This was a risky political move since racial profiling was a controversial topic. Yet it was precisely the type of issue that Obama seemed uniquely suited to address.

With his abilities as a lawmaker growing, Obama's career progressed rapidly. He next set his sights on the U.S. Senate as a new election approached. Obama hoped to extend his influence with a voice in the federal government.

Chapter Three

Storming
the Senate

Though he was still a state senator, Obama decided to take a risk and aim high. With valuable lessons from his unsuccessful bid for the House of Representatives, Obama was better equipped for his next political run. As he campaigned for the U.S. Senate, Obama used his biracial heritage to his advantage by connecting with diverse voters. Obama won the Democratic primary held in March 2004, earning 53 percent of the vote, more than all of the other Democratic candidates combined. He hoped that his hard work and the connections he forged with constituents would pay off in the general election that followed.

Facing Off with Ryan

Winning the Democratic primary was only half the battle. In the general election, Obama faced a formidable Republican opponent named Jack Ryan. Like Obama, Ryan was young and Harvard educated. He had earned a master's degree in business administration from Harvard Business School and a law degree from Harvard Law School. Moreover, like Obama, Ryan did more than talk about helping the underprivileged in urban Chicago. Ryan had left his lucrative finance job with Goldman Sachs to teach at an inner-city Chicago parochial high school.

Yet despite their similarities, Ryan and Obama were vastly different in terms of political philosophy. Ryan, more so than even the most conservative Republicans, believed in cutting taxes for all citizens, especially high-income earners. He was against gun control and abortion and in favor of school vouchers, which would enable parents to send their children to schools other than their own district's public schools to take advantage of better school systems.

Before the election took place, Ryan's campaign fell apart. Negative details about his relationship with his former wife, actress Jeri Ryan, became public as the result of custody proceedings. The scandal ruined Ryan's campaign and forced him to withdraw his candidacy for senator. This left the Illinois Republican Party scrambling for a replacement. Obama was already leading in the polls against Ryan, but now he was suddenly running unchallenged.

Another Challenger

With no Republican challenger to Obama, the Illinois State Republican Committee went beyond state borders to recruit a nationally known African American conservative named Alan Keyes. By this time, Obama's popularity was surging, so Keyes faced an uphill battle trying to convince Illinois residents to vote for him. This was especially difficult given the fact that he did not even live in their state. Nonetheless, the Maryland resident accepted the invitation to run against Obama.

As an African American conservative, Keyes drew attention to himself. Race was a major and complicated issue for Keyes because he rejected many beliefs widely held by other African Americans. For example, Keyes opposed affirmative action, a policy that requires state-funded institutions, such as universities and government agencies, to accept or hire a proportionate number of minorities.

Yet it was precisely because of his conservatism that Keyes was selected. The Illinois State Republican Committee believed he

Obama and Keyes engaged in televised debates as they campaigned for election in the 2004 Senate race.

could challenge Obama, whose more liberal opinions made for a sharp contrast between the two candidates. In fact, one of Keyes's strategies, much like Ryan's, was to portray Obama as radically liberal on the major issues. Yet while Keyes made shocking statements about his opponent within Illinois, Obama was about to be catapulted into the national spotlight.

The Democratic National Convention

By the summer of 2004, John Kerry, a senator from Massachusetts, had taken the lead in the Democratic presidential race and was about to face President George W. Bush in the general election. At the time, the Democratic Party had received criticism for not reaching out to African Americans. After meeting Obama,

Obama is shown here at the 2004 Democratic National Convention with John Kerry. During Obama's second term as president, he appointed Kerry to be secretary of state.

hearing him speak at a fund-raiser in Chicago and participating in a town hall meeting with him, Kerry was reportedly impressed with Obama's "passion, eloquence, and charisma," according to one of his aides. After Kerry's advisers predicted that Obama could someday be part of a national ticket, Kerry responded, "He should be one of the faces of our party now, not years from now."[27] The Kerry campaign then asked Obama to give the keynote address at the Democratic National Convention in July.

Obama recognized Kerry's invitation as an honor and a responsibility and wrote a speech that caught the attention of most of the nation. Often refrerred to by the title "The Audacity of Hope,"

Becoming a Best Seller

After he became president of the *Harvard Law Review*, Obama wrote a memoir titled *Dreams from My Father: A Story of Race and Inheritance*, published in 1995. However, it was not until his electrifying speech at the Democratic National Convention in 2004 that interest in Obama's life story and sales of the newly released paperback edition skyrocketed. In the book, Obama described his life growing up and evaluated his place in the world as the son of a Kenyan father.

Obama lost his mother to cancer soon after the 1995 edition was published. In the preface to the 2004 release, he wrote, "I think sometimes that had I known she would not survive her illness, I might have written a different book—less a meditation on the absent parent, more a celebration of the one who was the single constant in my life ... I know that she was the kindest, most generous spirit I have ever known, and that what is best in me I owe to her."[1]

1. Barack Obama, *Dreams from My Father: A Story of Race and Inheritance*. New York, NY: Three Rivers, 2004, p. xii.

the speech was one of the most memorable moments from the convention. In it, Obama spoke about how the nation's strength could come only from unity, not division:

Now even as we speak, there are those who are preparing to divide us, the spin masters and negative ad peddlers who embrace the politics of anything goes. Well, I say to them tonight, there is not a liberal America and conservative America—there is the United States of America. There is not a Black America and White America and Latino America and Asian America—there's the United States of America. The pundits like to slice-and-dice our country into Red States and Blue States; Red States for Republicans, Blue States for Democrats. But I've got news for them, too. We worship an awesome God in the Blue States, and we don't like federal agents poking around in our libraries in the Red States. We coach Little League in the Blue States, and yes, we've got some gay friends in the Red States. There are patriots who opposed the war in Iraq, and there are patriots who supported the war in Iraq. We are one people, all of us pledging allegiance to the Stars and Stripes, all of us defending the United States of America. In the end, that's what this election is about. Do we participate in a politics of cynicism, or do we participate in a politics of hope?[28]

Senator Obama

Political experts and many notable politicians weighed in favorably on Obama's performance. He exited the convention and won his own election against Keyes, receiving 70 percent of the vote while Keyes mustered only 27 percent. According to an analyst writing in the *Economist*, "Republicans may try to blame the result on Alan Keyes, their candidate who was hopeless; they may talk about the meltdown of the state's Republican Party; but they lost the race for the open Senate seat in Illinois for a much simpler reason. In Barack Obama, they were up against a star."[29]

On January 3, 2005, Obama was sworn in as a senator and a member of the 109th Congress while family and friends looked on from the visitors' gallery. Many people considered Obama's victory to be pure luck because of the misfortunes of his opponents. Although some of Obama's hardworking staff objected to this view, Obama himself said, "There was no point in denying my almost spooky good fortune."[30]

After achieving a landslide victory to become the junior senator of Illinois, Obama became an influential voice on Capitol Hill. As a rising star of the Democratic Party, he was often asked to

Obama celebrated his victory with his family after he won the 2004 Senate race.

comment on the policies and actions of President George W. Bush's Republican administration. Yet while he was at times an outspoken opponent of the president's decisions, Obama also proved his knack for working with members of the opposition party in the state of Illinois. His ability to communicate and compromise made a difference in the national debate on the most critical international and domestic issues of the day.

No issue at the time was as large as the war in Iraq, and Obama always vehemently opposed it. The Bush administration began the war in March 2003 in the belief that Iraq possessed weapons of mass destruction capable of threatening world peace. They also believed that the country's leader, Saddam Hussein, was harboring terrorists. Hussein was an oppressive dictator who ruled his people through intimidation and violence.

U.S. troops entered the city of Baghdad in 2003 and helped dismantle statues of the Iraqi leader, Saddam Hussein.

Though the Bush administration was successful in defeating Hussein, no weapons of mass destruction were ever found. Furthermore, there was no evidence linking Hussein and the terrorist group al-Qaeda. This group was led by Osama bin Laden, the mastermind behind the September 11, 2001, terrorist attacks on the World Trade Center and the Pentagon.

The war continued after Hussein's capture. It was not waged on a traditional battlefield with identifiable enemy lines. Instead, it was fought in a terror zone where numerous insurgent groups detonated bombs and shot at U.S. troops daily. The episodes of violence as Iraq scrambled to form its own democratic government dragged on with no end in sight. What was once an apparent victory had turned into a complex mess of warring tribes, with security far from certain. In a speech to the Chicago Council on Foreign Relations on November 22, 2005, Obama stated,

I think … that the [Bush] Administration launched the Iraq war without giving either Congress or the American people the full story … I strongly opposed this war before it began, though many disagreed with me at that time. Today, as Americans grow increasingly impatient with our presence in Iraq, voices I respect are calling for a rapid withdrawal of our troops, regardless of events on the ground.

But I believe that, having waged a war that has unleashed daily carnage and uncertainty in Iraq, we have to manage our exit in a responsible way—with the hope of leaving a stable foundation for the future, but at the very least taking care not to plunge the country into an even deeper and, perhaps, irreparable crisis. I say this not only because we owe it to the Iraqi people, but because the Administration's actions in Iraq have created a self-fulfilling prophecy—a volatile hotbed of terrorism that has already begun to spill over into countries like Jordan, and that could embroil the region, and this country, in even greater international conflict.[31]

Obama's predictions about the spread of violence and conflict in the region as a result of the continued chaos in Iraq seemed to be coming true in the summer of 2006. With neighboring Iran disregarding calls from the United States and the United Nations to dismantle its nuclear program and war waging between Israel and Lebanon, it appeared that relations between countries in the Middle East and the United States could be strained even further. Obama took a role in international diplomacy as a member of the Senate Foreign Relations Committee, which meant that he would be a key player in negotiations between the United States and countries that threatened world peace.

Passing Legislation

An important issue that led to the invasion of Iraq was the potential proliferation of weapons of mass destruction. To maintain world peace, the U.S. sought to remove the threat. They focused specifically on the materials used to produce such weapons. Obama worked closely with Senator Richard Lugar, a Republican from Indiana, to accomplish these goals.

In an effort to prevent makeshift weapons manufacturing, Obama and Lugar drafted S.2566, the Lugar-Obama Act. Introduced on April 6, 2006, its purpose was to expand the State Department's ability to detect and stop weapons and the development and trafficking of materials to create weapons of mass destruction. Specifically, the act would help secure lightweight antiaircraft missiles.

The potential threat of dangerous materials in the hands of terrorists is just one of the major international issues on which Obama focused. Another was the related subject of energy and oil production. These were among the most critical matters affecting American peace and economic prosperity.

A New Approach to Energy

Russia and the Middle East are often the focal points of U.S. foreign policy because these regions produce the vast majority of the world's oil. Oil fuels transportation and many industries in the United States, yet it often comes from other countries.

Obama's approach to solving the problem of U.S. dependence on foreign oil was two pronged: reduce consumption and fund initiatives to rapidly develop alternative fuel sources. He argued for the advancement of biofuels, such as ethanol, as well as other technologies that harness fuel from agricultural products. He said, "With technology we have on the shelves right now and fuels we can grow right here in America, by 2025 we can reduce our oil imports by over 7.5 million barrels per day—an amount greater than all the oil we are expected to import from the entire Middle East."[32]

In addition to developing incentives to make more fuel-efficient

In 2006, Senator Obama traveled to New Orleans, Louisiana, to help with efforts to rebuild and recover from the damage caused by Hurricane Katrina the previous year. Extreme storms like hurricanes can result from climate change.

cars, which would have a positive impact on the environment, Obama tried to enact legislation that would provide government funding for alternative fuel technologies that could halt the effects of global warming and climate change.

Scientific evidence confirms that Earth's climate is changing in dangerous ways, a problem that Obama tried to tackle from his days in the Senate through his presidency. The changes result from the excessive consumption of fossil fuels, used in practically every building, factory, home, and motor vehicle on the planet. The emissions from these fuels lead to higher-than-average tem-

Supporting Innovation

In June 2006, Barack Obama and Senator Jim Bunning introduced the Coal-to-Liquid Fuel Promotion Act of 2006. The legislation, which was never passed, would have created tax incentives for coal-to-liquids (CTL) technology and the construction of CTL plants, making CTL an environmentally friendly energy resource in the United States.

Coal is an abundant domestic resource. When gasified in the CTL process, it is refined into diesel. This final product is cleaner than regular diesel because of the removal of sulfur and nitrogen. According to Obama,

The people I meet in town hall meetings back home would rather fill their cars with fuel made from coal reserves in Southern Illinois than with fuel made from crude reserves in Saudi Arabia. We already have the technology to do this in a way that's both clean and efficient. What we've been lacking is the political will. This common sense, bipartisan legislation will greatly increase investment in coal-to-liquid fuel technology, which will create jobs and lessen our dependence on foreign oil. Illinois Basin Coal has more untapped energy potential than the oil reserves of Saudi Arabia and Kuwait combined. Instead of enriching the Saudis, we can use these reserves to bring a renaissance for Illinois coal.[1]

1. Quoted in Sourcewatch.org, "Statement by Obama on Introducing S.3325, the 'Coal-to-Liquid Fuel Promotion Act of 2006,' with Senator Jim Bunning (R-KY), in June 2006." www.sourcewatch.org/index.php?title=Barack_Obama_statements_on_coal.

peratures that are causing huge portions of ice to melt in places such as the North Pole, the South Pole, and Greenland. As the ice melts, water levels around the world will rise and coastlines will gradually be submerged. Additional problems may include abnormally warm temperatures and more frequent and powerful tropical storms and tornadoes.

While in the U.S. Senate, Obama was critical of the Bush administration's claim that there was no scientific proof of global warming. He pointed to countries that accepted global warming as scientific fact and changed their policies to reverse the effects. Obama pushed for legislation that would reduce harmful emissions from factories and provide incentives for companies to switch over to cleaner energy alternatives such as solar power. He also made strides toward supporting the improvement of cleaner ways to burn coal, which is the most abundant source of energy in the United States.

Working for Reform

In addition to energy and environmental issues, education was another of Obama's particular interests as a senator. With tuition costs rising at alarming rates, young Americans from middle- and lower-income families found it harder to afford college. Obama recognized the financial hardships and took steps to make education more accessible to everyone. In April 2005, he introduced the Higher Education Opportunity Through Pell Grant Expansion (HOPE) Act. Its purpose was to amend the Higher Education Act of 1965 and make college more affordable by increasing the maximum amount of Pell Grant awards by nearly 26 percent.

It was not only education at the college level that concerned Obama. He also committed to ensuring full funding of government-sponsored programs such as Head Start, which provides education, medical, dental, and parent-involvement programs to impoverished children and their families. Because of his commitments to early childhood education and to accessible, high-quality day care, Obama was the 2005 recipient of the Harold Blake Walker Award, which is given to individuals for their contributions to human services or social reform.

Whether the issue was education, energy, the environment, or foreign relations, in his first term as a U.S. senator, Obama focused his attention and efforts on key domestic and international issues that held tremendous significance for the future of the United States. Clearly, he was a leader with his vision trained on the horizon. Because of his farsighted, optimistic approach to politics, many people looking ahead to the 2008 presidential election had their eyes on Obama.

Chapter **Four**

From Senator to President

Barack Obama was a little-known state legislator until July 27, 2004, when he delivered the keynote address at the Democratic National Convention. Millions of people who watched him on television were mesmerized by his eloquence and the drama of his life story. His stirring words and his work as the fifth African American senator in U.S. history quickly transformed him into a political star and a potential candidate for the presidency.

On the Campaign Trail

Political groups around the country were anxious to meet Obama, who was making a name for himself as a charismatic and intelligent leader. In his first term as a U.S. senator, Obama quickly demonstrated his political savvy, his interest in making changes in Washington, and his willingness to work hard on issues important to him and the people who elected him to office. When a reporter asked him about his rapid rise to political prominence, Obama responded, "I think what people are most hungry for in politics right now is authenticity."[33]

By late 2006, many people were urging him to run for president. Obama was intrigued by the idea but realized the

Thousands gathered at the Old State Capitol in Springfield, Illinois, on February 10, 2007, to hear Obama announce his intention to run for president.

campaign posed many risks to himself and his family. He was not sure whether he could win, and a failed campaign would doom any future chance to be elected president. He also knew he would be the target of personal attacks that could hurt his family. When Obama eventually decided to enter the race, he instantly became one of the front-runners to win his party's presidential nomination.

On February 10, 2007, Illinois witnessed history as Obama made his intent to run for president official. Obama said he sought the Democratic presidential nomination because he was the only candidate who would dramatically change the domestic and foreign polices of President George W. Bush that were hurting the nation:

I recognize that there is a certain presumptuousness in this—a certain audacity—to this announcement. I know that I have not spent a long time learning the ways of Washington, but I have been there long enough to know that the ways of Washington have to change.[34]

The theme of "change" became the heart of Obama's campaign.

The Historic Campaign

The 2008 Democratic presidential campaign was historic because, if it was successful, it was likely that either a black or a female candidate would take office. Joining Obama in making history was New York senator Hillary Clinton, whose husband, Bill, had been president from 1993 to 2001. Obama and Clinton were the leaders among more than a half-dozen Democrats who were seeking the nomination.

In the first poll of candidates in November 2006, Clinton ranked first with 28 percent of likely voters and Obama second with 17 percent. Despite Obama's solid showing, many political analysts did not believe he could win. They cited his inexperience—he had been a senator for only two years. They also believed racism would deny him some white votes and weaken him too much to defeat Clinton. Even worse, as the first black candidate considered to have a chance to win, some supporters warned him that racists might try to assassinate him. There were death threats against him, and the U.S. Secret Service started protecting Obama in May 2007, eight months before the first primary.

Obama quickly showed his political strength by raising $24.8 million in the first quarter of 2007—more money than

With her experience as a senator and First Lady, Hillary Clinton was a strong candidate for president in 2008.

anyone except Clinton. He also drew huge, enthusiastic crowds to political rallies. Soon, the race became a clear battle between Obama and Clinton.

Challenging Clinton

Tension between the candidates began not long after Obama announced his candidacy. Throughout the state primaries, the Clinton campaign fought hard to regain its momentum after several important advances by Obama. Clinton and her husband viewed Obama as the biggest threat to a Clinton victory.

In her opposition, Clinton cited Obama's lack of experience and claimed that even though she had only been a senator a few years longer than Obama, she was much more prepared to be president. Clinton argued that her role as former First Lady gave her more White House and foreign policy experience. She called Obama's speeches, which were generating enthusiasm among voters, "just words."[35] The Clinton campaign also tried to argue

The Role of Racism

Political experts were surprised that being African American did not hurt Barack Obama in the 2008 presidential election, but Obama himself had predicted more than a year before the primaries began that race would not derail his candidacy. Obama said that even though racism against black people still existed in the United States, he was confident he could convince enough white voters to support him to win. In an interview with *Essence* magazine in October 2007, he said,

I don't believe it is possible to transcend race in this country. Race is a factor in this society. The legacy of Jim Crow [a century of Southern racism against blacks] and slavery has not gone away. It is not an accident that African Americans experience high crime rates, are poor, and have less wealth. It is a direct result of our racial history. [But] I think that racial attitudes have changed sufficiently in this country, that people are willing to vote for me for president, if they think I can help them on health care, on education, on the issues that are important in their lives. Now, are there going to be people who don't vote for me because I am black? Absolutely. But I do not believe those are people who would have voted for me, given my political philosophy, even if I were white.[1]

1. Quoted in Gwen Ifill, "The Candidate," *Essence*, October 2007, p. 226.

that Obama was elitist and out of touch with the majority of the black population.

Obama forcefully challenged Clinton in televised debates but mostly refrained from running negative political ads about her. Instead, he concentrated on telling voters what he would do to change U.S. policy, like ending the Iraq War, making health care more affordable, and discouraging political bickering between the Republican and Democratic Parties.

The Power of Positivity

Throughout his rivalry with Clinton, Obama kept faith in his ability to win. In a speech in Nashua, New Hampshire, Obama congratulated his opponent on her successes in the campaign. Then, Obama told cheering supporters he could still win the race:

> We will remember that there is something happening in America; that we are not as divided as our politics suggests; that we are one people; we are one nation; and together, we will begin the next great chapter in America's story with three words that will ring from coast to coast; from sea to shining sea — Yes. We. Can. [36]

Obama repeated the phrase "yes we can" over and over to explain his philosophy of political optimism and to give his supporters a sense of hope throughout the long march to Election Day. "Yes we can" became a mantra for his campaign, which was growing stronger across the nation thanks to thousands of people who were volunteering to work for him and donating money.

His hopes and confidence were rewarded. Obama accepted the Democratic nomination on August 28 in Denver, Colorado. He delivered a dramatic speech to 84,000 people jammed into a football stadium. Obama said he was ready to meet the greatest challenge facing the nation. The greatest challenge, however, was no longer the Iraq War, the overriding issue when the campaign began. Instead, it was the weakening U.S. economy, which Obama said was harming millions of people:

Positive themes of hope, change, and empowerment were hallmarks of Obama's 2008 presidential campaign.

Tonight, more Americans are out of work and more are working harder for less. More of you have lost your homes and even more are watching your home values plummet. More of you have cars you can't afford to drive, credit card bills you can't afford to pay, and tuition that's beyond your reach.[37]

Obama claimed he was better suited than Arizona senator John McCain, the Republican presidential candidate, to deal with the economy. The general election would be decided by whether or not voters believed that statement.

Talking Points

McCain posed a stark contrast to Obama. A Vietnam War hero hailed for his bravery as a prisoner after his plane was shot down, McCain wanted to keep American troops in Iraq. He had also supported President Bush's policies for eight years. Obama based his campaign on bringing American troops home from Iraq and overturning many Bush policies. There was also a disparity in the ages of the candidates. McCain was 72 years old, and many voters wondered if he could handle the stress of being president. If elected, McCain would be the oldest person to ever become president.

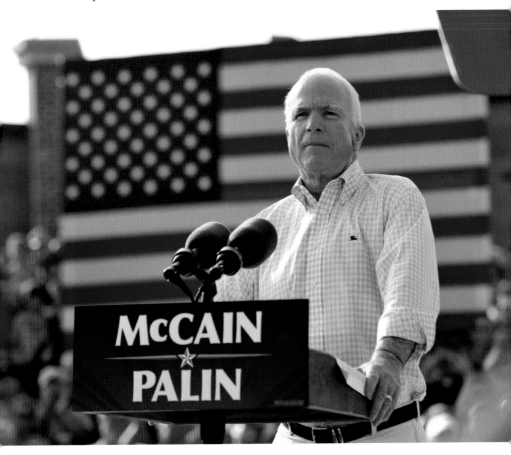

John McCain's military background and political history generated an immediate base of supporters.

Harnessing Technology

One of the biggest advantages Barack Obama had over his two main opponents—Hillary Clinton and John McCain—was his campaign's superior use of technology. The Obama campaign effectively harnessed the internet with the website www.barackobama.com, the most powerful political campaign site at that time. Once someone registered on the site, Obama's campaign kept emailing updates and requests for donations. That effort helped Obama raise a record $750 million, more than twice as much as McCain. The site also helped link his supporters in various states and around the country so they could get together and work for him. Social networking sites also helped Obama's campaign attract thousands of volunteers. Obama focused on communicating with MySpace and Facebook users and started a YouTube channel people could subscribe to and find out about the campaign.

Obama's campaign also used cell phones in new ways. When Obama picked Delaware senator Joe Biden as his vice presidential running mate, his campaign announced it first in text messages sent to supporters who had submitted their telephone numbers. Campaign organizers sent other news about the campaign and made appeals for donations via text. Obama's campaign also effectively used its main website and other sites to counter political attacks, often just a few hours after the attacks were made.

Obama announced that Joe Biden (shown here) would be his running mate on August 22, 2008, just before the Democratic National Convention began.

Rising discontent over the Iraq War and Bush's growing unpopularity gave Obama an early lead over McCain. Also, Obama was soon able to claim McCain did not understand the election's most important issue—the failing U.S. economy. At a rally in Jacksonville, Florida, on September 15, McCain admitted to about 300 people that "the American economy is in crisis [but] the fundamentals of our economy are strong."[38] This statement was perhaps the biggest mistake McCain made in his campaign.

McCain had been commenting on the latest development in the continuing deterioration of the economy—the collapse of Lehman Brothers, one of the nation's largest investment banks, and the sale of Merrill Lynch, another investment firm. Hours later at a rally in Pueblo, Colorado, Obama told 3,000 people that McCain's comment showed that he did not understand why the economic downturn happened.

The worst recession in eight decades was caused by a variety of factors, including the cost of gasoline (it soared to more than four dollars a gallon), home mortgage defaults that weakened banks, a huge decline in the value of stocks, and massive layoffs by financially troubled businesses. Those economic problems had become the top concern of voters. McCain's comment made it seem as if he did not realize how much the weakened economy was hurting people who were losing jobs, homes, and investment savings that they needed to live on. The result was that more voters began to believe Obama was better suited than McCain to salvage the economy.

The General Election

The race between Obama and McCain was expected to be close. However, by early fall, Obama was ahead in the polls. His advantage continued to expand as voters decided he was best suited to guide the nation. This growing lead allowed Obama to visit his 86-year-old grandmother, Madelyn Dunham, who was dying of cancer. In Honolulu that October, Obama praised the woman who had helped raise him: "She has really been the rock of the family, the foundation of the family. Whatever strength and discipline that I have, it comes from her."[39]

Although they were opponents, Obama and McCain showed respect for each other throughout their campaigns. When McCain passed away in 2018, Obama spoke at his funeral.

Obama was saddened when he had to return to the campaign because he knew he would probably never again see the woman he lovingly called "Toot," a shortened version of Tutu, the Hawaiian word for grandmother. She died on November 2, two days before her grandson won a landslide election to become the nation's first black president.

On November 4, Obama tallied about 69,456,000 votes (52.9 percent of those cast) and 365 electoral votes to 59,934,000 (45.7 percent) and 173 electoral votes for McCain. Political pundits credited Obama's win to several possible factors. The weakening economy was one factor. The United States seemed unified in a widespread desire for change after the Republican policies of

Obama and his family welcomed the enthusiasm of the crowd in Grant Park on election night.

the Bush administration. Many said that voters trusted Obama to turn the economy around and to restore hope.

The night he was elected, Obama addressed thousands of jubilant people at Grant Park in Chicago just a few miles from his Hyde Park home. He told them, "If there is anyone out there who still doubts that America is a place where all things are possible, who still wonders if the dream of our founders is alive in our time, who still questions the power of our democracy, tonight is your answer."[40]

Chapter Five

In the
White House

In the two months between the election and inauguration, Obama prepared for his new position. Choosing people to head key government agencies was his first order of business. His most surprising pick was Senator Hillary Clinton as secretary of state. He chose Clinton even though she had waged a tough campaign against him. Obama said she was the person best suited to help him deal with foreign policy issues. The choice signaled Obama's willingness to collaborate with former rivals and draw the best minds together in order to improve the country.

On January 20, 2009, Barack Obama was sworn in as the 44th president of the United States and the first African American to fill that role. In front of an estimated 1.8 million people—a record-breaking crowd—Obama delivered his first address as president. He vowed to tackle the problems facing the nation with a spirit of determination, collaboration, and unity. As president, Obama was burdened with a faltering economy and two foreign wars, but he stepped confidently into the Oval Office with the goal of building a stronger country. His election in 2008 and reelection in 2012 granted Obama eight years to turn his visions for the country into reality.

The historic election of an African American president was celebrated at the first Inaugural Ball. The president and First Lady danced into their new roles as Beyoncé performed.

Winning the Nobel Prize

Shortly after taking office, President Obama was awarded a great, international honor. He was chosen to receive the Nobel Peace Prize of 2009. Past winners include Nelson Mandela, the 14th Dalai Lama, Desmond Tutu, and other world and spiritual leaders who have made great strides toward world peace. Obama was chosen to receive the award for his collaborative and cooperative values in international politics. His commitment to making the world safe from nuclear weapons was recognized by the award. Coming at the very beginning of his presidency, the Nobel Prize set high expectations for Obama to meet in his future actions as a world leader.

Reversing Recession

Even before he was inaugurated, Obama began meeting with his advisers to find ways to help the nation's economy recover from its worst economic downturn since the Great Depression. Obama and his team crafted an $800-billion plan to help citizens struggling with financial problems, especially the more than 2 million people who had lost jobs. The new plan included income tax breaks, more money for unemployment benefits, and massive spending on domestic programs to create jobs.

Obama began building public support for the plan by discussing its importance in news conferences and public appearances before he became president. During a January 16, 2009, visit to a manufacturing plant in Bedford Heights, Ohio, Obama warned that swift action was needed to fix the economy: "It's not too late to change course—but only if we take dramatic action as soon as possible. The first job of my administration is to put people back to work and get our economy moving again."[41]

Obama submitted his proposal to Congress before he took office. Just eight days after he became president, the House passed the measure. The Senate passed the bill on February 10. The Senate and House then argued over the scope of the final legislation before finally agreeing on a $787-billion bill to help revive the nation's weakened economy. Obama signed the measure into law as the American Recovery and Reinvestment Act on

With Vice President Biden looking on, President Obama signed the economic stimulus bill aimed at steering the nation out of a recession.

February 17 in Denver, Colorado. It was the largest single expenditure of money in U.S. history.

Swift action on the economic stimulus bill had historians comparing Obama to President Franklin D. Roosevelt, who in 1933 initiated a flurry of bills in his first hundred days in office to help the nation recover from the Great Depression. Obama predicted the bill would begin helping Americans suffering from the financial downturn, but he had this reminder for Americans:

> *Now, I don't want to pretend that today marks the end of our economic problems. Nor does it constitute all of what we're going to have to do to turn our economy around. But today does mark the beginning of the end: the beginning of what we need to do to create jobs for Americans scrambling in the wake of layoffs, the beginning of what we need to do to provide relief for families worried they won't be able to pay next month's bills, the beginning of the first steps to set our economy on a firmer foundation, paving the way to long-term growth and prosperity.*[42]

Obama's stimulus bill was a short-term measure aimed at boosting the economy. Obama was also planning new programs to help the ailing industries and homeowners who were having trouble paying their mortgages. He granted financial support to General Motors and Chrysler in order to save the auto industry from collapse. He also bolstered large banks on the verge of bankruptcy by providing substantial loans. Obama took further measures to help American families suffering financially, from lowering mortgage costs to providing low-interest loans for small businesses.

Over the course of Obama's presidency, the economy slowly but steadily improved and another Great Depression was avoided. Unemployment fell from almost 10 percent in 2009 to less than 5 percent by 2017. This was due in part to the creation of 11.3 million new jobs in that time span. Wages grew, but so did income inequality. Though it was far from perfect, the economy President Obama left behind in 2017 was much stronger than the one he inherited in 2009.

Obamacare

At Obama's urging, the Senate approved a measure on January 29, 2009, to expand health coverage to more children. This was the beginning of one of the main hallmarks of Obama's presidency—a dogged pursuit of improved health care for all Americans. On the campaign trail, Obama had promised to reform health care. His Democratic predecessors Bill Clinton and Jimmy Carter had failed in their efforts for universal health care. As president, Obama would meet with more success, though it took a longer and more bitter battle than he anticipated to accomplish his goal.

In a spirit of collaboration and bipartisanship, Obama called together Democrats, Republicans, health care professionals, and representatives of the drug industry to help draft a bill. The resulting proposal was met with staunch opposition around the country. That summer, town hall meetings erupted with loud protests. Many of the bill's opponents belonged to the Tea Party, a rising group of Republicans with extremely conservative views. The Tea Party believed the government was overstepping its role by regulating health care. Opponents worried about losing their existing coverage, about the requirement that all Americans have insurance, and about the costs of the program at a time when the national budget was already strained. They assigned the term "Obamacare" to the reforms, a name that stuck with both opponents and proponents of the bill.

Obama appealed to the nation in a televised address on September 9, 2009. He explained that the reforms had three main goals. First, they would provide added security for those who already had health insurance. Second, they would provide insurance for the millions of Americans who did not have it. Third, they would work to keep health care costs from growing too quickly. Obama also tried to clear up mistaken notions about the bill, such as the idea that it would provide insurance to undocumented immigrants.

Because of Obama's determined advocacy for the bill, it was eventually signed into law as the Patient Protection and Affordable Care Act (often known as the ACA) on March 23, 2010. Early problems with the ACA-supported website posed further challenges to its

In the summer of 2009, surprisingly vigorous protests broke out across the country as fears about Obamacare took hold.

success and damaged its reputation. These initial problems were eventually resolved, and the program fully launched. The ACA still faced challenges once it was in action, but Obama and the courts managed to preserve its changes. The Supreme Court upheld its constitutionality, and Obama vetoed a Republican bill to repeal the act in 2016.

Although the ACA proved to be an uphill battle for Obama, it was successful in meeting his goals of insuring and providing improved care for citizens. As a result of the ACA, 30 million Americans gained health insurance. Millions more who had pre-existing conditions could not be denied coverage. In addition, young adults could remain on their parents' insurance until age 26. Throughout the long struggle, Obama held firmly to the idea that health care should be a right for all Americans.

However, after Obama left office in 2017, court cases and new legislation cast a long shadow of doubt about the long-term future of the ACA.

America at War

Obama had been a longtime opponent of the war in Iraq. He had pledged during his campaign to bring home the thousands of American troops stationed there. Once in office, Obama worked to keep that promise. He developed a plan in February 2009 and set a deadline of August 2010 for removing most troops from Iraq. He hoped to reduce the troops from 160,000 to 50,000 by that date. By 2012, Obama had succeeded in reducing American troops in Iraq to a mere 150.

Obama also worked on a plan to close the military prison at the U.S. Naval Station Guantánamo Bay in Cuba. The station had become controversial for holding Iraqi war prisoners without allowing them a chance to prove their innocence. Although he hoped to close Guantánamo within a year, this plan ultimately failed. Obama did succeed in reaffirming his stand against torturing military prisoners, though. Within his first 100 days in office, he delivered an executive order banning excessive interrogation techniques.

In Afghanistan, Obama sought to ensure that the Taliban was under control before withdrawing American troops. He worked with military advisers on a strategy for training Afghan

Throughout his presidency, protests urged Obama to keep his promise of closing the Guantánamo Bay prison and ending the torture of Iraqi prisoners.

forces in the meantime. Obama sent 33,000 additional troops to Afghanistan to help with this effort in 2009. He planned to end combat operations in August 2010 and start pulling out troops in July 2011. Although Obama found that the presence of American troops in Afghanistan was still necessary in 2015, their numbers had dropped significantly, from 97,000 in 2011 to 12,000.

Besides carrying out his campaign promises regarding the American military, Obama found an early opportunity to prove his skill and judgment as commander in chief. In 2011, military intelligence indicated that Osama bin Laden was hiding out at a compound in Pakistan. The al-Qaeda leader was credited with planning the September 11 attacks that resulted in almost 3,000 deaths. Obama met with his advisers and gathered as much information as possible about the potential consequences

The atmosphere in the Situation Room was tense as Obama and his team waited for the attack on bin Laden to unfold.

of an attack on the compound. The operation would be risky. It was uncertain whether or not bin Laden was present, and a secret military strike could threaten friendly relations between the United States and Pakistan, where the compound was located. After weighing the options, Obama ordered an attack. His gamble was rewarded with the capture and killing of Osama bin Laden on May 2, 2011, by a team of Navy SEALs. Bin Laden's death was significant and symbolic. It signaled to America and the world that Obama would be decisive and forceful in the fight against terrorism.

Fierce Opponents

Obama had moved quickly in fulfilling his campaign promises about the economy, health care, and the war in Iraq. In his first two years in office, he also passed legislation on other important issues, such as the fight for equal pay for women. However, Obama soon hit a brick wall when it came to passing legislation.

Republicans had been stalwart opponents of nearly all of Obama's proposals from the beginning. His appeals for bipartisanship had been routinely rejected. When the economic stimulus plan passed, not a single Republican voted for it. When the ACA passed, only three Republican senators voted in its favor. Every Republican in the House of Representatives voted against it. Obama had narrowly scraped by in passing these bills with the help of the Democratic majority in Congress. However, conditions were about to change. In the midterm election of 2010, Obama's advantage was lost when Republicans took control of the House of Representatives.

Despite the disapproval of Republicans who thwarted his legislation whenever possible, Obama decided to seek reelection in 2012. This time, his opponent was Mitt Romney, the former governor of Massachusetts. Obama again used grassroots organizing to fuel his campaign and focused on advancing the gains he had made since 2008, but Romney was a formidable opponent. Nevertheless, Obama secured the election, winning by 5 million votes with 60 percent of the electoral college. He had again earned the votes of the majority of African

The first bill Obama signed was a new law making it easier for workers to sue for pay discrimination. The Lilly Ledbetter Fair Pay Act of 2009 aimed to narrow the gender pay gap.

Americans, Latinx people, and Asian Americans, but he attracted fewer white voters than in 2008.

Approaching a second term in office, Obama committed himself to enhanced gun control, energy alternatives, immigration reform, protection for same-sex marriage, and continued economic growth. With the House of Representatives controlled by Republicans, the odds of passing legislation were stacked against him. In 2014, the balance shifted even further as Republicans gained the majority in the Senate. Congress was under Republican control, but Obama still devoted himself to the issues he had championed in his campaign. He used a variety of executive powers, including vetoes, executive

Barack Obama took the oath of office for a second time on January 21, 2013.

orders, proclamations, and regulations, in order to work toward his goals.

Support for DACA

One of the immigration reforms that Obama continued to support despite Republican resistance was Deferred Action for Childhood Arrivals (DACA). Obama created the policy in 2012. This policy provides a route to safety for undocumented immigrants who came to the country before they were 16 years old. It allows qualifying immigrants to have deportation hearings delayed for two years. In some cases, the two years can be renewed. The act also allows the covered immigrants to work in the United States in the meantime. Obama created the measure after the DREAM Act, which would have provided a path to citizenship for the same immigrants, failed to pass in Congress.

Gun Control

Just a month before his second inaugural address, Obama experienced what he called his worst day in office. On December 14, 2012, an armed man entered Sandy Hook Elementary in Newtown, Connecticut, and killed 20 students and 6 adults. This was not the first mass shooting since Obama became president, but he was deeply moved by the tragedy. Obama reached out to the families of Newtown at a prayer vigil two days after the shooting and vowed to do better. He said:

In the coming weeks, I will use whatever power this office holds to engage my fellow citizens—from law enforcement to mental health professionals to parents and educators—in an effort aimed at preventing more tragedies like this. Because what choice do we have? We can't accept events like this as routine. Are we really prepared to say that we're powerless in the face of such carnage, that the politics are too hard? Are we prepared to say that such violence visited on our children year after year after year is somehow the price of our freedom?[43]

In the wake of the mass shooting, Obama acted to pass stricter gun control laws. He proposed key changes to existing laws. The first was a requirement for universal background checks. Background checks are a tool for blocking people with a criminal history from buying guns. If they were universal, it would mean that no one could buy a gun without a background check first. The second was a ban on the sale of assault weapons and high-capacity magazines. Obama also called for greater protections for schools and a renewed focus on treating mental illness across the country. The National Rifle Association (NRA) along with vocal Republicans and some Democrats objected to the proposals. When a bill for wider background checks was rejected in 2013, Obama said that it was "a pretty shameful day for Washington."[44]

Obama addressed another tragic mass shooting in 2015 after a gunman killed nine African Americans at a church service in Charleston, South Carolina. The president delivered the eulogy for Reverend Clementa Pinckney, a state senator killed in the attack. Again, Obama called for greater gun control, referring to Newtown, a shooting at a movie theater in Aurora, Colorado, and the most recent attack in South Carolina:

For too long, we've been blind to the unique mayhem that gun violence inflicts upon this nation. Sporadically, our eyes are open: When eight of our brothers and sisters are cut down in a church basement, 12 in a movie theater, 26 in an elementary school. But I hope we also see the 30 precious lives cut short by gun violence in this country every single day; the countless more whose lives are forever changed—the survivors crippled, the children traumatized and fearful every day as they walk to school, the husband who will never feel his wife's warm touch, the entire communities whose grief overflows every time they have to watch what happened to them happen to some other place.[45]

Obama drew attention to gun violence around the country and the race discrimination that exacerbated it. The shooting in Charleston was a hate crime against African Americans, and Obama recognized that violence within and against black communities was a persistent and tragic problem in America. Unable to pass gun reform in Congress, Obama instead took executive action in 2016. He passed expanded background checks, improved reporting of lost and stolen guns, offered mental health care improvements and information sharing about mental health issues, and encouraged research into smarter gun technology and safety features. Obama said, "Until we have a Congress that's in line with the majority of Americans, there are actions within my legal authority that we can take to help reduce gun violence and save more lives—actions that protect our rights and our kids."[46]

Climate Change

Climate change loomed as another undeniable threat during Obama's administration, and he took clear steps to counter its worst effects. Heeding the scientific evidence of a changing climate that had motivated him as a senator, Obama continued to promote environmentally smart innovations. He lobbied for changes that would cut carbon emissions and pushed for alternative energy sources. Obama viewed renewable energy not only as a way to ensure the future but also as a means of boosting the economy. Solar and wind power were sources of new employment opportunities for Americans. In his 2013 inaugural address, just months after Hurricane Sandy ravaged the East Coast, Obama affirmed:

We will respond to the threat of climate change, knowing that the failure to do so would betray our children and future generations. Some may still deny the overwhelming judgment of science, but none can avoid the devastating impact of raging fires and crippling drought and more powerful storms.

The path towards sustainable energy sources will be long and sometimes difficult. But America cannot resist this transition, we must lead it. We cannot cede to other nations the technology that will power new jobs and new industries, we must claim its promise. That's how we will maintain our economic vitality and our national treasure—our forests and waterways, our crop lands and snow-capped peaks. That is how we will preserve our planet, commanded to our care by God.[47]

Obama again developed his environmental agenda with executive actions. In 2015, he vetoed a bill that would allow the Keystone XL Pipeline to carry oil across the country, from Canada

In November 2015, Obama posed with other international leaders in Paris as they committed to proactive environmental policies.

to the Gulf of Mexico. That same year, he developed a Clean Power Plan to limit carbon pollution, especially from coal, and to set state and national goals to use more renewable energy in the future.

The historic Paris Climate Conference also took place in 2015, with Obama playing a key role. This gathering of almost 200 countries invited participants to reduce their national carbon footprint and fund the research and development of alternative energy. The agreement they reached offered the opportunity for the world's nations to hold each other accountable for creating a cleaner future. On behalf of the United States, Obama promised to cut 25 percent of its emissions by 2030. The resulting agreement was ratified on October 5, 2016, and took effect the following month.

Equal Rights

Although Obama faced a rigid gridlock in Congress, he had managed to influence the laws of America through his Supreme Court appointments. In 2009, Obama appointed Sonia Sotomayor as the first Latina justice on the Supreme Court. The following year, his appointment of Elena Kagan was also accepted. These two liberal-leaning judges contributed to many important rulings over the course of Obama's presidency and beyond. One of those important decisions came about in 2015.

The ruling of the *Obergefell v. Hodges* civil rights case upheld the fundamental right of same-sex couples to marry. It declared that the right is guaranteed by the 14th Amendment, which insures the equal protection of the law to all citizens. As a result, the *Obergefell v. Hodges* decision made it possible for same-sex couples to be married in all 50 states.

Obama had already proved himself an ally of the LGBT+ community long before this ruling. In his first term, Obama repealed the Bush-era "Don't Ask, Don't Tell" policy for gay members of the military. The ACA made it illegal for insurers to turn away LGBT+ people. In 2013, Obama refused to support the Defense of Marriage Act, which offered a narrow definition of marriage as a union between a man and woman. He continued to speak out for

The night of the historic *Obergefell v. Hodges* decision, Obama lit up the White House in rainbow colors.

equal rights for LGBT+ citizens and against their discrimination in all areas of life, including health care, housing, and employment. Obama celebrated the momentous strides toward marriage equality made in 2015, saying, "When all Americans are treated as equal, we are all more free."[48]

Foreign Relations

Limited in the changes he could make domestically, Obama often turned his attention to foreign relations throughout his two terms. From the very beginning of his presidency, Obama had begun working to heal relations with Muslim countries, which had deteriorated because of the Iraq War. In his first interview as president, Obama said that he would open talks with Muslim nations and others that opposed the United States, a diplomatic tactic Bush had shunned.

Obama held to his promise by historically reaching out to the government of Iran. It had been 30 years since the U.S. government made direct contact with Iran. However, Obama saw an opportunity to build a relationship between the two nations, and he initiated a phone call with the Iranian president Hassan Rouhani in 2013. The presidents began negotiations on a deal that would limit Iran's nuclear program in exchange for lifting some of the sanctions on Iran. Sanctions are penalties meant to punish a dangerous or threatening country.

The Iran Nuclear Deal was completed in July 2015. As a result, inspectors would be allowed to enter the country and confirm that Iran was upholding the agreement and not creating nuclear weapons. In return, the United States and other countries could begin interacting economically, culturally, and diplomatically with Iran again.

Obama also turned his attention to Cuba, another country that had been a historic adversary of the United States. After a 50-year period without diplomacy between the two countries, Obama began to forge a new relationship in 2014. His goal was to eventually open travel and commerce between the United States and Cuba. In 2016, Obama made a historic visit to the island nation. It was the first time a sitting president had been to Cuba since 1928. Obama and Cuban president Raúl Castro discussed human rights, Guantánamo Bay, and the U.S. embargo, or ban, on trade with Cuba. The embargo could not be lifted without approval from Congress, but both presidents were hopeful for a stronger relationship in the future.

Unfortunately, not all of Obama's foreign dealings were as positive or cooperative as the new arrangements with Iran and Cuba. Obama also called for military strikes and interventions around the world. Shortly after the attack on Osama bin Laden's compound in Pakistan, Obama sent forces to support rebels in Libya. They helped topple the Libyan dictator Muammar al-Qaddafi in 2011. Obama opted for special forces strikes and bombings instead of sending ground forces to Libya. This tactic was used again in other counterterrorism campaigns. Obama favored the use of drones when possible in foreign attacks. Drones are controlled remotely and can be used for surveillance and to drop bombs.

Obama used similar tactics to counteract the rise of the Islamic State in Iraq and Syria, or ISIS, in 2014. This radical group took root along the border of Syria and Iraq, engaging in terrorist activities. That year, ISIS released a video showing the beheading of two American journalists. Obama reacted with a battery of airstrikes in Syria, added American troops in Iraq, and appealed to the United Nations for support. These actions resulted in heightened counterterrorism activities and a dramatic rise in Syrian refugees seeking safe harbors around the world. The threat of terrorism and its effects at home and abroad was a persistent theme throughout Obama's presidency.

The Way Forward

As the 2016 presidential election approached and Obama's time in office drew to a close, he placed his full support behind Hillary Clinton, the Democratic candidate for president. In his official endorsement, the president claimed, "I don't think there's ever been someone so qualified to hold this office."[49] Obama hoped that the programs he created and gains he made in office would be secured and expanded under Clinton's leadership.

Instead, Republican Donald Trump's victory in the electoral college placed many of Obama's advances in danger. Trump's platform stood in exact opposition to Obama's work as president. Where Obama had sought security for the children of undocumented immigrants, Trump's main campaign promise was to build a wall along the Mexico border. Where Obama worked to provide health insurance for millions of Americans, Trump planned to repeal the ACA immediately. Where Obama put his faith in clean energy, Trump supported the expansion of the coal industry.

Knowing that many of the executive actions he had taken could be easily reversed by the new administration, Obama called for the support of the American people. He wrote and published articles before leaving office that focused on the issues he felt were most important. In "The Irreversible Momentum of Clean Energy," published in *Science*, Obama argued for the importance of clean energy. He called on citizens, businesses, and industries to back renewable sources even if Trump pulled out of the Paris Climate Agreement. In an article for the *New England Journal of Medicine*, Obama urged Congress and president-elect Trump to improve rather than dismantle the ACA. He argued that an immediate repeal would leave millions of Americans without necessary care.

In his last days in office, Obama took a stand for criminal justice reform by pardoning individuals convicted of federal crimes. Throughout his presidency, he pardoned 212 offenders and lightened the sentences for 1,715 more, including 504 life sentences. On January 19, 2016, he lessened 320 sentences for nonviolent, drug-related crimes. Obama used this constitutional power more frequently than other presidents, especially at the end of his presidency.

Obama delivered his farewell address on January 10, 2017, in Chicago. He expressed his gratitude for the honor of serving as president and congratulated the nation on its achievements over the past eight years:

> *If I had told you eight years ago that America would reverse a great recession, reboot our auto industry, and unleash the longest stretch of job creation in our history—if I had told you that we would open up a new chapter with the Cuban people, shut down Iran's nuclear weapons program without firing a shot, take out the mastermind of 9-11—if I had told you that we would win marriage equality and secure the right to health insurance for another 20 million of our fellow citizens—if I had told you all that, you might have said our sights were set a little too high.*

> *But that's what we did. That's what you did. You were the change. The answer to people's hopes and, because of you, by almost every measure, America is a better, stronger place than it was when we started.*[50]

Chapter Six

Life
After Office

A s Donald Trump took the oath to serve as the 45th president of the United States, it became apparent that many of the trends and policies advocated by Obama would be reversed. Obama encouraged the American people to speak for their interests, engage fully in democracy, and use the tools preserved and provided in the U.S. Constitution and the Bill of Rights.

Meanwhile, the Obama family settled into a quieter, more private routine. They left the White House for another home in Washington, D.C., so that Sasha could finish high school.

In the months and years after finishing their second term, the Obamas signed a joint book deal with Penguin Random House. The former First Lady's book, *Becoming*, immediately joined best-seller lists after its publication in 2018. Obama started handwriting the first draft of his book after leaving office. It will likely be released in the midst of the 2020 presidential campaign. The political memoir is expected to expand on the themes of personal growth, family history, and political reform developed in Obama's other two books, *Dreams from My Father* and *The Audacity of Hope*.

As storytellers, the Obamas also hope to influence wider audiences with their company Higher Grounds Productions.

A 2018 deal between Higher Ground and Netflix will result in the creation of documentaries, feature films, and series on the streaming service. The stories are intended to inspire, inform, and entertain.

Outside of the White House, Obama has found new avenues for advancing the key reforms he championed throughout his term of public service. He has been a featured speaker at many events and continues to pursue diplomacy. International trips and collaborations with world leaders and former U.S. presidents have been hallmarks of Obama's post-presidency period.

Race Relations

When Obama was elected president, some called the moment the beginning of a "post-racial" America. Obama's victory stunned many who had believed racism was still too strong in the United States for a black person to be elected president. Some considered Obama's election proof that the nation had become less racist. Many people also believed Obama's presidency would further improve the nation's racial climate. In a magazine article published in October 2007, Obama himself had speculated on the effect his election could have:

> As president, obviously the day I am inaugurated, the racial dynamics in this country will change to some degree. If you've got Michelle as first lady, and [daughters] Malia and Sasha running around on the South Lawn [of the White House], that changes how America looks at itself. It changes how White children think about Black children, and it changes how Black children think about Black children.[51]

On the day of Obama's inauguration, Tyreese Holmes claimed Obama's victory had already had a positive impact on his sons, 12-year-old Malik Williams and 10-year-old Jalen Williams. Holmes, an African American, had taken them to Centennial Olympic Park in Atlanta, Georgia, to watch the historic event on a giant screen. Holmes told a reporter that Obama's election had already raised his expectations for what his sons could accomplish. He said, "The sky's the limit for them now. Malik talks about being an astronaut, and seeing [Obama] become president, [now] I can encourage him to be an astronaut. It feels like anything is possible."[52]

This hopeful attitude was threatened by events such as the shooting of Trayvon Martin in 2012, the rise of police violence and racial profiling that stimulated the Black Lives Matter movement in 2013, and the Charleston, South Carolina, hate

The portraits of Barack and Michelle Obama are now on display at the Smithsonian's National Portrait Gallery in Washington, D.C.

crime against African Americans in 2015. Over the course of Obama's presidency, it became clear that race relations were far from harmonious in America. Still, the election and reelection of the first African American president was a monumental and symbolic step toward racial equality.

A Place in History

On February 12, 2018, the official portraits of Michelle and Barack Obama were unveiled at the National Portrait Gallery in Washington, D.C. Not only were these the first presidential portraits to feature African Americans, they were the work of black artists. New York artist Kehinde Wiley painted the former president's portrait against a backdrop of greenery and vibrant blooms native to Chicago, Kenya, and Hawaii to symbolize Obama's background and heritage. The former First Lady's likeness was captured in muted tones by Baltimore-based artist Amy Sherald. The installation of the portraits marked an important moment when the stories of Barack and Michelle Obama were entered into the long history and legacy of the American people.

Barack Obama's legacy will also be commemorated by the Obama Presidential Center. This campus is slated to be built in Chicago's South Side neighborhood as a way to record Obama's historic presidency and revitalize and support the area of Chicago where Obama put down roots as an adult. Plans for the center include community gathering spaces and a museum, public library, and athletic center.

Throughout American history, leaders have come from unlikely places and unexpected circumstances. From his beginnings as a self-described "skinny kid with a funny name" to his global significance as president of the United States, Obama relied on hard work, determination, and thoughtfulness to reach his goals. In reaching his own goals, he broadened the path for the people following behind him. In his post-presidency years, Obama can be expected to integrate the lessons of his time in office with new insights that promote the march toward greater justice and equality in America.

Notes

Introduction: Making History

1. Barack Obama, "The Challenges We Face Are Real," *Milwaukee Journal Sentinel*, January 21, 2009.

2. Quoted in Diane Ravitch, *The American Reader: Words That Moved a Nation.* New York, NY: HarperCollins, 1991, p. 20.

3. Obama, "The Challenges We Face Are Real."

4. Quoted in Ravitch, *The American Reader*, p. 334.

5. Quoted in Dahleen Glanton, "Living King's Dream on the National Mall," *Chicago Tribune*, January 21, 2009.

Chapter One: Humble Beginnings

6. Barack Obama, *Dreams from My Father: A Story of Race and Inheritance.* New York, NY: Three Rivers, 2004, p. 15.

7. Obama, *Dreams from My Father*, p. 17.

8. Obama, *Dreams from My Father*, p. 126.

9. Obama, *Dreams from My Father*, p. 51.

10. Obama, *Dreams from My Father*, p. 52.

11. Obama, *Dreams from My Father*, pp. 69–70.

12. Quoted in *O, The Oprah Magazine*, "Oprah's Cut with Barack Obama," November 2004. www.oprah.com/omagazine/20 0411/omag_200411_ocut.jhtml.

13. Obama, *Dreams from My Father*, pp. 79–80.

14. Obama, *Dreams from My Father*, p. 99.

15. Noam Scheiber, "Race Against History," *New Republic*, May 31, 2004, p. 22.

Chapter Two: An American Experience

16. Obama, *Dreams from My Father*, p. 115.

17. Obama, *Dreams from My Father*, p. 134.

18. Obama, *Dreams from My Father*, p. 136.

19. Obama, *Dreams from My Father*, p. 139.

20. Obama, *Dreams from My Father*, pp. 164–165.

21. Obama, *Dreams from My Father*, p. 242.

22. Scott Turow, "The New Face of the Democratic Party—and America," Salon, March 30, 2004. dir.salon.com/ story/news/ feature/2004/03/30/obama/index.html.

23. Quoted in Amanda Ripley, "Obama's Ascent," *TIME*, November 15, 2004, p. 74.

24. William Finnegan, "The Candidate," *New Yorker*, May 31, 2004.

25. Quoted in Scheiber, "Race Against History," p. 22.

26. Turow, "The New Face of the Democratic Party—and America."

Chapter Three: Storming the Senate

27. Quoted in Jill Zuckman and David Mendell, "Obama to Give Keynote Address," *Chicago Tribune*, July 15, 2004.

28. Barack Obama, Keynote Address at Democratic National Convention, Boston, MA, July 27, 2004. p2004.org/demconv04/ obama072704spt.html.

29. *Economist*, "Obama's Second Coming: Victory for a Rising Star," November 6, 2004, p. 33.

30. Barack Obama, *The Audacity of Hope: Thoughts on Reclaiming the American Dream*. New York, NY: Crown, 2006, p. 9.

31. Barack Obama, Address to Chicago Council on Foreign Relations, Chicago, IL, November 22, 2005. obamaspeeches.com/040-Moving-Forward-in-Iraq-Chicago-Council-on-Foreign-Relations-Obama-Speech.htm.

32. Barack Obama, Address to Governor's Ethanol Coalition, Washington, DC, February 28, 2006. obamaspeeches.com/054-Energy-Security-is-National-Security-Governors-Ethanol-Coalition-Obama-Speech.htm.

Chapter Four: From Senator to President

33. Quoted in Ripley, "Obama's Ascent," p. 76.

34. Barack Obama, Announcement of Presidential Candidacy, Springfield, IL, February 10, 2007. content.time.com/time/nation/article/0,8599,1588045-2,00.html.

35. Quoted in David Von Drehle, "The Five Faces of Barack Obama," *TIME*, September 1, 2008, p. 32.

36. Barack Obama, Speech at New Hampshire Primary, Nashua, NH, January 8, 2008. www.scoop.co.nz/stories/WO0801/S00115/barack-obama-yes-we-can-thank-you-new-hampshire.htm.

37. Barack Obama, Acceptance of Nomination at Democratic Convention, Denver, CO, August 28, 2008. www.npr.org/templates/story/story.php?storyId=94087570.

38. Quoted in Carol E. Lee, "McCain Says Fundamentals of Economy Strong Despite Threat," *Gainesville (FL) Sun*, September 16, 2008.

39. Quoted in Robert Barnes, "Obama Visits Grandma Who 'Was His Rock,'" *Washington Post*, October 25, 2008, p. A-2.

40. Barack Obama, Election Night Acceptance, Grant Park, Chicago, IL, November 4, 2008. edition.cnn.com/2008/POLITICS/11/04/obama.transcript/.

Chapter Five: In the White House

41. Quoted in *Milwaukee Journal Sentinel*, "Obama Wants Green Economy," January 17, 2009.

42. Quoted in Sheryl Gay Stolberg and Adam Nagourney, "Recovery Measure Becomes Law and Partisan Fight Endures," *New York Times*, February 18, 2009, p. A17.

43. Barack Obama, Remarks at Sandy Hook Prayer Vigil, Sandy Hook, CT, December 16, 2012. www.npr.org/2012/12/16/167412995/transcript-president-obama-at-sandy-hook-prayer-vigil.

44. Quoted in Jeff Wallenfeldt and David Mendell, "Barack Obama," *Encyclopaedia Britannica*, May 15, 2019. www.britannica.com/biography/Barack-Obama/The-2012-election.

45. Barack Obama, Eulogy for Clementa Pinckney, Charleston, SC, June 27, 2015. www.cnn.com/2015/06/27/politics/obama-eulogy-clementa-pinckney/index.html.

46. Quoted in "Standing with the President for Smart Gun Laws," Giffords Law Center, January 5, 2016. lawcenter.giffords.org/standing-with-the-president-for-smart-gun-laws.

47. Barack Obama, Second Inaugural Address, Washington, DC, January 21, 2013. obamawhitehouse.archives.gov/the-press-office/2013/01/21/inaugural-address-president-barack-obama.

48. Quoted in Scott Neuman, "Obama: Supreme Court Same-Sex Marriage Ruling a 'Victory for America,'" NPR, June 26, 2015. www.npr.org/sections/thetwo-way/2015/06/26/417731614/obama-supreme-court-ruling-on-gay-marriage-a-victory-for-america.

49. Quoted in Annie Karni, "President Obama Endorses Hillary Clinton," Politico, June 9, 2016. www.politico.com/story/2016/06/president-obama-endorses-hillary-clinton-224130.

50. Barack Obama, Farewell Address, Chicago, IL, January 10, 2017. obamawhitehouse.archives.gov/farewell.

Chapter Six: Life After Office

51. Quoted in Gwen Ifill, "The Candidate," *Essence*, October 2007, p. 226.

52. Quoted in Judy Keen, "Feelings Reach Heightened Pitch in USA," *USA Today*, January 21, 2009.

Barack Obama Year by Year

1961
Barack Hussein Obama Jr. is born in Honolulu, Hawaii, on August 4.

1979–1981
Obama attends Occidental College in Los Angeles, California.

1983
Obama graduates from Columbia University in New York City.

1983–1987
Obama works as a community organizer in Chicago, Illinois.

1990
Obama becomes the first African American president of the *Harvard Law Review*.

1991
Obama graduates magna cum laude from Harvard Law School in Massachusetts.

1992
Obama directs a voter registration drive in Chicago and marries Michelle Robinson.

1995
Obama's memoir, *Dreams from My Father: A Story of Race and Inheritance*, is published.

1996
Obama is elected to the Illinois state senate.

1997–2004

Obama as an Illinois state senator.

2000

Obama runs unsuccessfully in the Democratic primary for Illinois's First Congressional District against incumbent representative Bobby Rush.

2004

Obama gives the keynote address at the 2004 Democratic National Convention in Boston, Massachusetts, on July 27; his memoir is rereleased in paperback.

2005

Obama is sworn in as a U.S. senator for Illinois on January 3. In April, he proposes his first Senate bill, the Higher Education Opportunity Through Pell Grant Expansion Act of 2005 (HOPE Act).

2006

Obama publishes his second book, *The Audacity of Hope*, on October 17.

2007

Obama launches his presidential campaign in Springfield, Illinois, on February 10.

2008

Obama wins the Iowa caucus on January 3, accepts the Democratic nomination for president on August 28, and is elected president of the United States on November 4.

2009

Obama is sworn in as the 44th president of the United States on January 20 and signs the American Recovery and Reinvestment Act on February 17.

2010

Obama signs the Affordable Care Act into law on March 23.

2011

Obama announces that Osama bin Laden was killed in a military strike on May 2.

2012

Obama wins reelection as president of the United States on November 6.

2014

The Obama Foundation, a Chicago-based nonprofit, is founded in order to train and support local and global leaders.

2015

The Supreme Court rules that the Constitution protects the right to same-sex marriage on June 26.

2016

The Paris Climate Agreement is ratified with support from the United States on October 5.

2017

Obama delivers his farewell address in Chicago on January 10. Obama takes part in a peaceful transfer of power to the 45th president on January 20.

2018

The Obama Foundation hosts its second annual summit in Chicago for scholars, leaders, and community members from around the world.

2019

Seven programs to be created through the partnership between the Obamas' company, Higher Grounds Productions, and Netflix are announced.

For More Information

Books

Neal, Anthony. *The Oral Presidency of Barack Obama*. Lanham, MD: Lexington Books, 2018.
Neal's thorough analysis of Obama's presidency in this book is supported with rich texts from Obama's most illuminating speeches.

Obama, Barack. *The Audacity of Hope: Thoughts on Reclaiming the American Dream*. New York, NY: Crown, 2006.
In this book, Obama recounts his early experiences as a senator and explains his vision of more authentic politics.

Obama, Barack. *Dreams from My Father: A Story of Race and Inheritance*. New York, NY: Three Rivers, 1995.
In this memoir, Obama discusses his life growing up with his mother and grandparents in Hawaii and his attempts to connect with his African heritage and identity despite the absence of his Kenyan father.

Obama, Michelle. *Becoming*. New York, NY: Crown, 2018.
In her first memoir, the former First Lady traces her journey alongside Barack Obama from the South Side of Chicago to the White House.

Souza, Pete. *Obama: An Intimate Portrait*. New York, NY: Little, Brown & Co. 2017.
In this book, Souza's photographs of Obama in the White House chronicle the history of his presidency in vivid detail.

Websites

Biography.com
(www.biography.com/us-president/Barack-Obama)
This site offers an up-to-date biography of Barack Obama with several videos of important public addresses.

Encyclopedia Britannica: Barack Obama
(www.britannica.com/biography/Barack-Obama)
This thorough overview of Obama's presidency also contains links to additional helpful information.

The Office of Barack and Michelle Obama
(www.barackobama.com)
Updated with news about the couple, this site provides resources related to their continued efforts for change in America.

On the Issues: Every Political Leader on Every Issue
(www.ontheissues.org)
This website provides information about America's past and present leaders and their positions on various issues.

The White House: President Barack Obama
(obamawhitehouse.archives.gov)
This website provides information about Barack Obama's presidency and an archive of his speeches while in office.

Index

Picture Credits

Cover Courtesy of the Library of Congress; p. 7 Jonathan Torgovnik/Getty Images; p. 17 Dimas Ardian/Bloomberg via Getty Images; p. 19 Helen H. Richardson/The Denver Post via Getty Images; p. 23 Laura S. L. Kong/Getty Images; p. 24 Thomas Grauman/Corbis via Getty Images; pp. 30, 63 Saul Loeb/AFP/ Getty Images; p. 32 Steve Liss/The LIFE Images Collection via Getty Images/Getty Images; pp. 33, 45 Scott Olson/Getty Images; p. 34 Lane Turner/The Boston Globe via Getty Images; p. 37 AP Photo/Frank Polich; p. 41 Jeff Roberson-Pool/Getty Images; p. 42 David Hume Kennerly/Getty Images; p. 46 Gilles BASSIGNAC/ Gamma-Rapho via Getty Images; p. 49 AP Photo/Rob Carr; p. 54 AP Photo/Brian Kersey; p. 56 Charles Ommanney/Getty Images; p. 59 Olivier Douliery/Abaca Press/MCT via Getty Images; p. 60 Gino Santa Maria/Shutterstock.com; p. 61 K2 Images/Shutterstock.com; p. 64 Joe Raedle/Getty Images; p. 66 Win McNamee/Getty Images; p. 68 AP Photo/Gerald Herbert; p. 71 Education Images/Universal Images Group via Getty Images; p. 72 Chip Somodevilla/Getty Images; p. 73 Pete Souza/ The White House/MCT via Getty Images; p. 75 Brooks Kraft LLC/Corbis via Getty Images; p. 76 Mark Makela/Corbis via Getty Images; p. 80 Ian Langsdon/AFP/Getty Images; p. 82 Drew Angerer/Bloomberg via Getty Images; p. 88 Mark Wilson/ Getty Images.

About the Author

Rachael Morlock lives in Western New York. She writes fiction and nonfiction books for children and young adults. Rachael is the author of the biography *Mary Cassatt: Famous Female Impressionist*, also published by Lucent Press.